GLASGOW RANGERS:
THE JOURNEY

The Acknowledgements

FIRST OF all, a big thank you to all those who helped make a fledgling idea become reality. This book is the end product.

Jeff Holmes worked his magic on the words and brought to life some of the stories portrayed in the pages of this book using his own unique insights as a Rangers fan. Without his input and advice this book would have been all pictures and no story.

My friend Richard Parker had the initial idea for the book and badgered me about it every time we met at a game.

Picture editors Ian Dawson of the *Express* and Blair Stewart of the *Sunday Mail* gave me invaluable support, without which I would not have been able to document all the games. Thanks for the continued use of my images in your publications.

Fellow photographer Keith Campbell from the *Scottish Sun* spent many long hours and miles with me as we travelled to away games and generally put the world to rights in our own inimitable way. He also deserves special thanks for the day I was stuck solid on the M6 as Mark Warburton and Davie Weir were about to be unveiled at Ibrox. His constant updates and abuse on the phone were invaluable – he is some wingman!

Wattie Cheung, Oban's no 1 snapper in exile, assisted with images from Sandy Jardine's march on Hampden. Thank you.

My long-suffering wife Susan has still not divorced me. One day we will have a nice holiday away which is not cut short and doesn't share a pre-season destination with Rangers!

And a special mention to Carol Patton, Stephen Kerr, Rodger McKelvie and other colleagues past and present at Rangers, thank you all for your help over the years.

To everyone else who assisted me, bought pies and shouted from the terraces, thanks for your patience and good humour.

For all the Rangers fans who contributed their memories of The Journey to this book, thank you. Your efforts were well received and very much appreciated.

And finally, a special mention of my mum, Muriel, who lost her brave battle with cancer during the dark days of our Division Three campaign. Driving from the Elgin match to reach her bedside at Raigmore Hospital, Inverness, is a journey I never want to make again. This book is for her.

GLASGOW RANGERS:
THE JOURNEY

MISSION
ACCOMPLISHED

Photographs by **Willie Vass**
Words by **Jeff Holmes**

First published by Pitch Publishing, 2016

Pitch Publishing
A2 Yeoman Gate
Yeoman Way
Worthing
Sussex
BN13 3QZ
www.pitchpublishing.co.uk
info@pitchpublishing.co.uk

A CIP catalogue record is available for this book
from the British Library.

ISBN 978-1-78531-251-9

Typesetting and origination by Pitch Publishing

Printed by Bell & Bain, Glasgow, Scotland

Contents

Introduction

A STAGGERING 220 matches, and 300,000 images shot over the length and breadth of the country, and beyond. That was The Journey for Willie Vass, photographer. And guess what? I wouldn't have missed a second of it for the world.

I first focused my lens on a Rangers match in 1986 as a fresh-faced teenager, recently moved to Glasgow, and thought this would be the perfect way for a cash-strapped university student to follow his team, practice his hobby and maybe earn some money on the side submitting match photos to Rangers. Imagine the thrill when I eventually earned a place on the staff of the Rangers News.

One of my first assignments for the 'News' was the inaugural Comic Relief Red Nose Day. I was dispatched to Ibrox at lunchtime with a big bag of red noses. I cautiously poked my head into the dining room and was promptly booted down the marble staircase, scattering plastic props all over the place! Subsequent assignments were more successful and I have enjoyed sharing the good and the bad times with the club and the fans.

For the past 25 years I have freelanced for all the major papers. I have covered Rangers through the highs of the Nine in a Row period, to the low point of Valentine's Day 2012 when Craig Whyte plunged the club into administration and set in motion the events which led to Rangers being kicked down to the basement of Scottish football.

Glebe Park. Ramsdens Cup. Peterhead. We had some new places to visit and there was quite some planning to do.

Did they even have mobile coverage in these places, I joked. How would I get my pictures sent – Wi-Fi or carrier pigeon? I needn't have worried for without exception all the SFL clubs during that first season were both welcoming and accommodating. They relished having the Rangers coming to town, and all who travelled to faraway places like Elgin, Annan, Forres and Berwick made it a day out.

I had a personalised pie left for me on my return to Borough Briggs, after poking fun at their matchday dining experience the first time around.

One club janitor even handed me the keys as I was taking so long sending pictures and told me to lock up and pop them through the letterbox on my way out!

Looking back through all the images it still seems incredible that a club the size of Rangers was forced to climb back through the lower leagues. Watching from gently sloping back gardens in Forres, from deckchairs on a garage roof in Angus or from halfway up a floodlight above a sodden hedge, the faithful Rangers fans arrived in huge numbers boosting the coffers of the small clubs and filling their local pubs and eateries.

We were sunburned pre-season in Brora, frozen to the bone in Cowdenbeath, snowed off at Ibrox, drenched in Ayr and blown away at Ochilview.

I attended every game on The Journey, although one of the final fixtures almost led to a divorce when Rangers re-arranged a match against Dumbarton for a Tuesday evening. We had booked a family holiday for that free week, and I was aghast when I realised this would potentially be the Championship-winning match. What was I to do but abandon my long-suffering wife and kids and travel back up to Ibrox on

Willie Vass

my own after only two nights away. And, of course, it did turn out to be the match that clinched promotion back to the Premiership.

The fans are the lifeblood of the club, so I hope in some small way this book and collection of images therein documents the way they followed their team as they travelled together on a long journey through Scottish Football's outposts to regain their rightful place back at the top.

Willie Vass
October, 2016

Administration

FROM THE day Rangers slumped depressingly into administration, Valentine's Day, 2012, to the moment they clinched promotion back to the Premier League, exactly four years, one month and 20 days elapsed.

There were times when it felt a great deal longer.

One season in Division Three, a solitary campaign in League One, and a couple in the Championship were negotiated before a 1-0 win over Dumbarton, on Tuesday 5 April, thanks to a James Tavernier goal, confirmed 'The Journey' was coming to an end.

But to understand how Rangers ended up plying their trade deep within the murky depths of Scottish football, we need to rewind to the 2010/11 campaign.

Even then, Rangers had started the new season with a degree of uncertainty due to the club's apparent rocky financial position. The summer months had started with a mass clear-out, and 15 players in total – including Nacho Novo, DaMarcus Beasley, Kris Boyd and Kevin Thomson – left the club.

It was clear early on that Walter Smith would have to operate on a smaller than usual budget, and he was soon forced to choose between quantity and quality. He opted for the latter, no doubt hoping for a relatively injury-free run.

It was a tough campaign, but Rangers won their last four games – scoring 16 goals in the process – to chalk up a third successive title; turning the tables on rivals Celtic, who had won three in a row immediately beforehand.

Rangers edged Celtic by a solitary point, and it was enough to land a record 54th league crown.

In February of that season, Scottish football's worst-kept secret, that Ally McCoist – Smith's assistant – would take over the Ibrox hot seat at the end of the season, was confirmed.

Rangers had played 55 competitive games, and also won the League Cup, but Smith's final season was perhaps notable for the signing of three players during the winter transfer window. David Healy, Kyle Bartley and El Hadji Diouf arrived at Ibrox – and not a penny changed hands. A sign of things to come?

But it seemed the perfect way for the legendary gaffer to leave the building, and with McCoist taking over, it was the dawning of a new era – although little did we know of the dangers lurking just around the corner.

McCoist's time as manager is well documented elsewhere within these pages, and even though his side blew a 15-point lead at the top of the Premier League in his debut season, there is no other manager in the history of the Rangers who was forced to endure what he did, with the constant battling and squabbling behind the scenes for control of the club quite clearly taking their toll.

At the tail end of season 2010/11, 6 May to be exact, Rangers chairman Sir David Murray sold his controlling interest, 85.3 per cent, in the club to businessman Craig Whyte for the princely sum of £1. The club now belonged to Wavetower Ltd, a company owned by Whyte. Wavetower was subsequently renamed The Rangers FC Group Ltd, and Rangers' huge debt to Lloyds Bank transferred to this company. Craig Whyte then deposed Alastair Johnston as chairman on 24 May.

An enduring image of the period will remain the sight of Whyte strolling purposefully along Edmiston Drive towards the main door at Ibrox, feted by supporters as the new saviour. Looks, or rather, individuals, can quite often be deceiving.

Paul Murray had already left, and boardroom upheaval continued throughout the close season with Martin Bain leaving his position as chief executive on 20 June, followed down the marble staircase later that year by the player once voted the Greatest Ever Ranger, John Greig, and fellow non-executive director John McLelland (not to be confused with the ex-player of the same name).

It was against this trouble-torn backdrop that McCoist was asked to prepare his squad for the new season, and midway through that campaign, on 13 February 2012, the unimaginable happened when Whyte took the decision to file legal papers at the Court of Session, serving notice of his intention to appoint administrators. Twenty-four hours later, on St Valentine's Day, Rangers officially entered admin and appointed Duff & Phelps as administrators.

A few days later, a Dean Shiels goal gave Kilmarnock a 1-0 victory in front of more than 50,000 supporters at Ibrox. But despite the defeat, and another couple in their next three games, things were still looking far more promising on the field than off it.

By entering administration, though, Rangers were docked ten points, which effectively ended their Premier League challenge.

Suddenly, the perennial battle with Celtic was the least of their worries. Whyte had filed for administration because of money owed to HM Revenue and Customs (HMRC), who had tried to appoint their own administrator prior to Duff & Phelps being given the nod. HMRC lodged its initial petition over alleged non-payment of around £9m in PAYE and VAT following Whyte's takeover.

When questioned about the club being placed in administration, Whyte said Rangers would 'come out stronger' and 'always be here'. Sadly that wasn't the way most fans were beginning to feel.

Paul Clark and David Whitehouse from Duff & Phelps were appointed joint administrators, and took over the day-to-day running of the club, with their priority to address a mounting debt problem. At the time, Clark said: 'All stakeholders involved with Rangers are working hard to ensure the long-term future of this national institution.'

He added: 'We have been working closely with HMRC in recent months to achieve a solution to the club's difficulties. However, this has not been possible due to ongoing losses and increased tax liabilities that cannot be sustained.

'We are working together with management and its major creditors, including HMRC, to achieve a solution to the financial problems which will ensure the ongoing survival of the business, which is of paramount importance to all concerned.

'We would like to take the opportunity of thanking fans for all their past and present support and hope we can rely on them in the future.'

A spokesman for HMRC said: 'We can't discuss specific cases for legal reasons but tax that has been deducted at source from the wages of players and support staff must be paid to HMRC. Any business that fails to meet that basic legal requirement puts the survival of the business at risk.'

In a statement, Whyte said HMRC's move meant the club had to 'accelerate' its plans, and added: 'The administrators are in and looking at everything and I will work with them to help them all I can and we'll have a plan to get out of administration by CVA [Creditors' Voluntary Agreement] as quickly as possible.

'Rangers will always be here. We will come out stronger and a better business and most importantly in a position to put as good a team as we can on the pitch and to win trophies which is what we all want as Rangers fans.'

Meanwhile, in Edinburgh, Murray admitted he was 'hugely disappointed' at the club's decision to appoint administrators and expressed surprise at the timing of the decision, while Sports Minister Shona Robison said Rangers' current plight was 'a concerning situation for everyone involved in Scottish football'.

Strathclyde Police were also monitoring the situation, especially with regards to policing at the next home game, but received guarantees from administrators that they would be paid for services provided.

It was worrying times for the club, and these fears were exasperated when it was claimed that Whyte had borrowed up to £24m against four years of future season ticket revenue from ticketing firm Ticketus.

Whyte was believed to be Rangers' secured creditor, and had acknowledged that the club had a £10m deficit in annual running costs, but most serious of all was the wait for the outcome of a tax tribunal decision over a disputed bill, plus penalties, totalling £49m.

Whyte reportedly said that this potential liability to HMRC could reach up to £75m if the club lost the tribunal.

HMRC believed the Ibrox club owed cash over its use of Employment Benefit Trusts (EBTs) to pay staff over a ten-year period. It alleged the Ibrox club did not administer the scheme properly and underpaid tax – a claim disputed by Rangers.

As secured creditor of Rangers, Whyte would have to be paid first ahead of others such as HMRC.

However, as a holder of 25 per cent or more of the club's debt, HMRC was in a position to block a creditors' agreement, which was necessary for Rangers to exit administration. If a creditors' agreement couldn't be reached – and the club couldn't be sold – it was possible Rangers could be wound up. It was crunch time for Rangers and its supporters.

And then came the next body blow – liquidation.

In mid-October 2012, creditors were said to have approved an end to the administration process, which led to Duff and Phelps applying to the Court of Session to have the club liquidated.

Following the blocking of a CVA by HMRC, which would have allowed the club to continue in administration, Duff & Phelps oversaw a sale of assets to a consortium led by Yorkshireman Charles Green for £5.5m.

It was then announced Rangers would take their place in the Scottish Third Division.

Meanwhile, Green personally oversaw the sale of season tickets for the 'start of a new era'. He delivered cups of tea and coffee to supporters queuing for tickets, and generally came across as an all-round good guy.

He challenged the football authorities at every turn, which was welcomed by fans more used to the Murray regime's limp-wristed attempts at publicly defending the club.

Was this indeed the dawning of a bright new era for Rangers? A new beginning after more than a century of plying their trade in the country's top flight? Supporters gobbled up season tickets for a trip into the relative unknown. For many thousands it was simply a matter of continuing their hands-on support for the club, while for others, perhaps lapsed fans, it was a call to arms in an hour of need.

As almost 40,000 bluenoses filed into Ibrox for a midweek cup tie against East Fife – their first home game on the lower league journey

– there was a definite air of optimism. A resignation that no longer would Rangers be dining at the top table had been accepted. The Journey was beginning and supporters decided to embrace it, get it over with and return to where they belonged as soon as possible.

Little did they know the nightmare was just beginning and many, many dark days – and shady characters – would follow.

Kris Boyd was one of the high-profile players to leave at the start of the 2010/11 season

Ally McCoist is unveiled as the new Rangers manager

Ally McCoist – in his playing days

*Ally McCoist and old
mentor Walter Smith
share a laugh*

Craig Whyte, second from right between police horses, walks down Edmiston Drive after his takeover of Rangers

A wave to supporters as Whyte 'enters the building'

Charles Green, right, and Imran Ahmad brief the media on their first day as club owners

A message of hope!

The Copland Road end is packed for the game against East Fife

Chapter One
The Journey Begins

THE PROBLEMS we had encountered during the previous six months, namely administration and liquidation, left the team and followers of the club fair game for criticism and banter from opposition fans, but I'm sure no one expected to roll up at Glebe Park for the first game of the season to find Brechin manager Jim Weir describing Rangers as a 'new club' within the pages of the official match programme. It was a cheap shot.

On the following page, City chairman Ken Ferguson welcomed Rangers to Glebe Park for 'only the second time in history'. Manager and chairman singing from different hymn sheets!

Ian Black and youngster Lewis Macleod made their competitive debuts for the Light Blues and after extra time Ally McCoist's side edged it by two goals to one, with Andy Little and Lee McCulloch on the scoresheet.

Walking up towards the ground that Sunday afternoon was surreal. It was the end of July, so we all knew it wasn't the Scottish Cup. That was when reality kicked in. Rangers were in the Ramsdens Cup; the competition for lower league teams. That's why we were starting off the season while players at SPL clubs still had their feet up or were playing glamour friendlies.

But after all the nonsense of the summer months, supporters were just glad to be back watching football – and Rangers – again. And judging by the crowd at Brechin, 4,123, the fans were buying into the trawl through the lower leagues.

But the acid test for supporters, and a game that would gauge perfectly just how popular a Division Three Rangers would be, came in the first home game of the season, a League Cup tie against East Fife, managed by old Gers favourite, Gordon Durie. Supporters had been used to watching the best on a weekly basis. Laudrup, Gascoigne, Goram, Gough. That was the calibre of player the last couple of generations had been brought up on. Absolutely no disrespect to the Class of 2012/13, but they weren't up to the usual standard of what the punters, myself included, were used to.

Still, this wasn't about the players, this was about the club, and early predictions that around 25,000 would pay in to the match were soon kicked into touch when supporters started arriving at the ground to see a queue the length of Sauchiehall Street outside the ticket office.

Personally, I wouldn't have missed it for the world. I hadn't been regularly for a couple of seasons, but this was my team and they needed my support. My season ticket was already safely tucked away in its wee plastic 'Rangers Till I Die' wallet – and I even managed to convince my wife to come along!

Well, the kick-off was held up to let the crowd in and when Lee McCulloch eventually got the game under way, there were more than 38,000 supporters in the ground. It was a sight that made us all extremely proud and, right there and then, we knew we could count on the magnificent Rangers supporters to steer us through these stormy waters. Rangers won 4-0, but that was hardly important.

A few days later, the bandwagon rolled on to the north east, Peterhead to be exact, and the beginning of the Scottish Third Division campaign. Thankfully, there were no 'digs' in the match programme and everyone of a Light Blue persuasion received a warm welcome in the 'Blue Toon'.

Mind you, perhaps it was that afternoon when most people realised the team was in for a bumpy ride in the third division, and that the opposition wasn't going to just roll over when they played the famous Glasgow Rangers, especially in front of their own supporters.

Rangers' historic first ever visit to Balmoor Park was a tousy affair and goals from Little and Barrie McKay ensured a solitary league point in a 2-2 draw.

It was going to be a long and arduous season, with visits to these 'soccer outposts' the norm rather than the exception. Along the way there would be choruses of 'You're Not Rangers Anymore', 'Sevco' etc, but by and large our supporters were welcomed with open arms wherever they went.

Ten of the 11 clubs in the Premier League had voted to banish the Blues to the third division in the name of sporting integrity, but when SPL panic set in, and noises were made about returning Rangers to the top flight with immediate effect, Ibrox fans overwhelmingly voted to remain where they were. The turkeys had voted for Christmas, and Rangers were quite happy to dine with their new comrades in the Scottish Football League. It would be an interesting journey.

Arriving at Brechin for the first match on The Journey

Programme with the
controversial manager's
notes

New Brazilian Emilson Cribari in the Ibrox
stand

Lee McCulloch scores the opener
against East Fife

Welcome to Peterhead

Ally McCoist at the dressing room door in Balmoor Park – 90 minutes later the smile was gone!

Carlos Bocanegra leads out Rangers at Peterhead

Neil Alexander pulls off a stunning save to deny Peterhead

Has Chris 'Waddle' just signed for Peterhead?

The Sky commentary team of Ian Crocker and Andy Walker perched high up on the Peterhead roof

The ball just misses the commentators!

Chapter Two

The Players

A TOTAL of 66 players – from 16 different countries – made a contribution, large and small, to The Journey. From that first league match at Peterhead, when it felt as though we were doomed to spend the rest of our existence outwith the top flight, to the midweek win over Dumbarton in April 2016, which sealed an albeit belated return to the Premier League, it was quite a trek.

Many of those from the 'League of Nations' made what could be termed 'minor contributions', while others – such as Lee Wallace and Lee McCulloch – were up there on 134 and 96 league appearances respectively.

But, to a man, they all played their part in helping us reach our goal, and each should be remembered for that. One of the early highlights of The Journey was the emergence of young Lewis Macleod. While naturally still a bit rough round the edges, it was crystal clear he was a fantastic prospect, and the type of youngster we should have been looking to build future teams around. But after just 20 league appearances he suffered a horrific knee injury in a largely forgettable 1-1 draw at home to Montrose in January 2013. He was out till the last day of the campaign.

The following season, and with a good pre-season under his belt, he started unbelievably well and scored four times in a seven-match spell, with the pick of the bunch undoubtedly his overhead kick against Ayr United at Somerset Park.

There was no stopping the Wishaw youngster and Scotland under-21 honours followed, but again his season was cruelly cut short in January when an adverse reaction to a virus affected the muscles close to his heart. Sadly, Macleod, who was just 19 at the time, wouldn't kick another ball that season.

The player made another determined comeback, but was on the receiving end of yet more bad luck in a match against Alloa just before Christmas, 2014, when he suffered a serious hamstring injury. By this time, Macleod had become a firm favourite with supporters for his natural ability, his goals and the courage he had showed in battling back from a number of setbacks.

But this meant very little to our board of directors who sold him to English Championship side Brentford for a reported fee of around £850,000, way below the player's valuation. The transfer went down like a lead balloon in the Ibrox stands, and protests against the board were stepped up. Meanwhile, Macleod insisted Rangers had made no attempt to keep him at Ibrox. The board had obviously sold him to the first interested club. The youngster did, however, insist he would like to return to Rangers later in his career.

Meanwhile, Canadian youngster Fraser Aird was another given an opportunity to play in the first team, no doubt due to the transfer embargo imposed on our club. I recall the talented wide boy coming on as a substitute in a league game against Queen's Park at Hampden, a few days after Christmas, 2012, which was attended by more than 30,000 Gers fans. The game was locked at 0-0 and Aird scored to make it seven wins out of seven in December.

Darren McGregor made a total of 46 appearances for the Light Blues during their ill-fated Championship season, and on each occasion he left everything he had out on the pitch. The defender, brought to Ibrox from St Mirren, won both the Player of the Year and Players' Player of the Year awards in his solitary campaign, and was rather surprisingly moved on as soon as new gaffer Mark Warburton arrived at the club.

And then there was Ian Black. He wasn't at all popular with Gers' fans prior to his move to Ibrox, due to a crunching challenge on Nikica Jelavic in a match between Rangers and Hearts at Tynecastle in October 2010, but when the diminutive midfielder made his Scotland debut against Australia at Easter Road, he was the target of abuse from Scotland fans. Rangers supporters were quick to back their player.

When Mark Warburton became manager, he naturally brought in a number of his own players, and all settled in quickly to become a big hit with the fans. However, few were as popular as Andy Halliday, the lad born a stone's throw from the Copland Road stand. When Halliday kissed the badge, you knew it was a genuine act of love.

James Tavernier was born a few hundred miles south of Ibrox, in Bradford, but quickly showed just how much the club meant to him, and his goalscoring exploits from the right-back position endeared him instantly to the Ibrox faithful. Long may Tav's goals continue, and the Yorkshireman be a part of the set-up at Ibrox.

But to rewind to the 'early days', it's hard not to remember the guy who started the ball rolling with the first goal on The Journey – take a bow Andy Little! Grabbing the first goal in the Ramsdens Cup first round tie at Brechin means the Northern Irishman will forever be a part of our long and illustrious history, and Little, who always gave 100%, deserves it as much as anyone else.

So, it was a collective effort that saw Rangers eventually move back up to the Premier League, and we can only hope the building blocks are now in place to ensure the club never again has to endure the trials and tribulations of the past four-and-a-half years.

Fraser Aird (62 league appearances, 9 league goals), Neil Alexander (36, 0), Anestis Argyriou (20, 0), Dominic Ball (21, 0), Cammy Bell (48, 0), Ian Black (85, 5), Carlos Bocanegra (3, 0), Kris Boyd (32, 3), Kirk Broadfoot (2, 0), Liam Burt (2, 0), Nicky Clark (83, 20), Darren Cole (3, 0), Robbie Crawford (46, 6), Emilson Cribari (33, 0), Jon Daly (53, 23), Sebastian Faure (49, 1), Shane Ferguson (2, 0), Wes Foderingham (36, 0), Harry Forrester (11, 4), Richard Foster (44, 0), Scott Gallacher (3, 0), Calum Gallagher (5, 1), Luca Gasparotto (4, 0), Dorin Goian (2, 0), Andy Halliday (35, 5), Ryan Hardie (6, 2), Chris Hegarty (25, 1), Kane Hemmings (5, 1), Jason Holt (32, 10), Kyle Hutton (47, 2), Rob Kiernan (33, 0), Billy King (12, 1), Kevin Kyle (8, 2), Nicky Law (92, 20), Andy Little (49, 27), Lewis Macleod (52, 11), Kyle McAusland (4, 0), Lee McCulloch (96, 38), Darren McGregor (41, 5), Barrie McKay (67, 7), Kenny Miller (65, 22), Andy Mitchell (7, 0), Bilel Mohsni (46, 11), Andy Murdoch (23, 1), Kal Naismith (17, 1), Nathan Oduwa (15, 1), Michael O'Halloran (12, 3), Arnold Peralta (24, 1), Ross Perry (17, 0), Lee Robinson (7, 0), Francisco Sandaza (15, 2), Dean Shiels (95, 20), Steve Simonsen (20, 0), Steven Smith (29, 3), Daniel Stoney (3, 0), James Tavernier (36, 10), Charlie Telfer (1, 0), David Templeton (67, 21), Jordan Thompson (2, 0), Haris Vuckic (21, 8), Martyn Waghorn (25, 20), Lee Wallace (134, 17), Tom Walsh (12, 0), Danny Wilson (30, 1), Marius Zaliukas (25, 2), Gedion Zelalem (21, 0).

Top 10 'Journey' appearances:
134: Lee Wallace, 96: Lee McCulloch, 95: Dean Shiels, 92: Nicky Law, 85: Ian Black, 83: Nicky Clark, 67: Barrie McKay, David Templeton, 65: Kenny Miller, 62: Fraser Aird, Kenny Miller.

Lee Wallace: Record appearances on The Journey

Top 10 'Journey' goalscorers:
38: Lee McCulloch, 27: Andy Little, 23: Jon Daly, 22: Kenny Miller, 21: David Templeton, 20: Nicky Clark, Nicky Law, Martyn Waghorn, 17: Lee Wallace, 11: Lewis Macleod, Bilel Mohsni.

Lewis Macleod relaxes on Ventura Pier in the USA

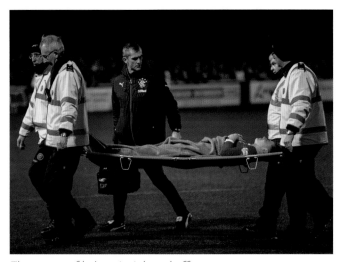

The agony of being stretchered off

The youngster celebrates his goal against St Johnstone

Fraser Aird takes the acclaim of the Rangers support

A personal message for midfield dynamo Ian Black

James Tavernier has been a revelation at Ibrox

Andy Halliday is a lifelong Rangers supporter

Andy Little celebrates the first goal on The Journey – at Brechin's Glebe Park

Youngster Robbie Crawford made 46 lower league appearances for Rangers

Newcastle United loanee Haris Vuckic had a deadly left foot

Goal king Nicky Clark signs for the Light Blues

Martyn Waghorn was one of Mark Warburton's first signings – and proved an excellent piece of business

Player of the Year 2014/15 was Darren McGregor

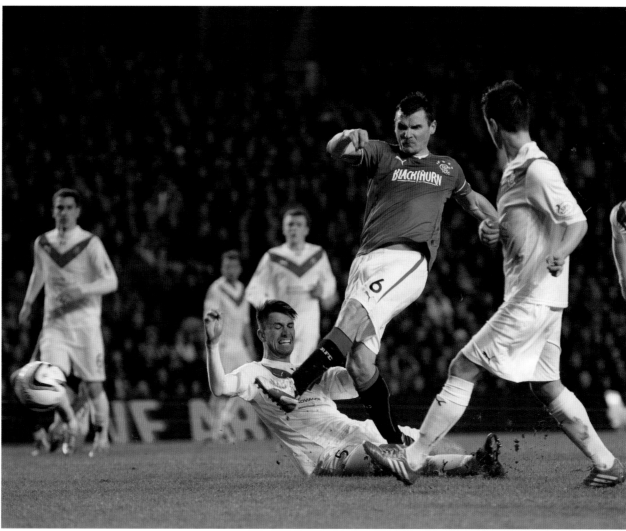

Lee McCulloch was Rangers' top scorer on The Journey

Chapter Three

The Gaffer #1 – Ally McCoist

WITH THE benefit of hindsight, was one man/manager ever going to be sufficient to drag us back from the brink of despair and destruction?

There's no doubt Ally McCoist will always be a Light Blues legend in the eyes of the Rangers support, if only for the amazing regularity with which he found the back of the opposition net. In 15 years as a player at Ibrox, he scored 355 goals, with his phenomenal haul of 49 in season 1992/93 an obvious highlight. And then there are the winners' medals. Ten championships, nine League Cups and a Scottish Cup between 1983 and 98. It doesn't get much better. But what about Ally the manager? By the time he left the club in the middle of the 2014/15 campaign, with his tired and well-beaten squad languishing in third place in the Championship title race, and a gaggle of points behind runaway league leaders Hearts, he would cut a forlorn figure on touchlines up and down the country. He was a tired man and it was time to go, more so for the good of his health than anything else. McCoist had taken over the first-team reins from long-time mentor Walter Smith: a seven-year apprenticeship leaving the 'golden one' as the perfect choice to inherit the throne. Or so it seemed. Sadly, it never quite worked out that way.

In his first season in charge – in the Premier League – McCoist presided over early eliminations from both the Champions League and UEFA Cup, thus denying a financially fragile ownership revenue which was no doubt counted upon to help the club survive a turbulent early period of stewardship.

However, the league campaign started brightly enough, and with players such as Allan McGregor, Steven Davis and Steven Whittaker signing contract extensions, a fourth successive league title certainly didn't seem out of the question. Especially when after an opening day 1-1 draw with Hearts, Rangers won their next nine league fixtures, an impressive run which included a 4-2 win over Celtic. A further three wins and two draws followed before Kilmarnock became the first club to lower the colours with a 1-0 win at Rugby Park.

Meanwhile, McCoist's first signing was the unspectacular Spanish midfielder Juan Manuel Ortiz from perennial sunshine strugglers Almeria.

By early October, McCoist's men were ten points clear of Celtic, and a month later that lead had been increased to 15 points over our Old Firm rivals, who were third, three points adrift of second placed Motherwell.

Celebrations, of a kind, were inevitable. It was a massive and surely unassailable lead. McCoist was proving to have the Midas touch for management, and Rangers were on course for four-in-a-row – and then it all went pear-shaped.

A draw with St Johnstone and subsequent defeats to Kilmarnock, St Mirren and Celtic saw the wheels fall off the wagon. Celtic embarked on a run of 21 matches undefeated which pushed Rangers down to second, where the Light Blues stayed for the rest of the season.

It was the most spectacular of on-field implosions, played out against a backdrop of off-field problems.

Administration and liquidation are documented elsewhere in this book, and when Rangers were thrown out of the Premier League, discarded like a journeyman player way past his prime, the supporters looked to McCoist and former Barcelona Bear, Sandy Jardine, who had taken on a senior ambassadorial role at the club, to guide them through the troubled waters.

It was a new dawn for the club, they were in uncharted territory, and while a whole host of unscrupulous 'businessmen' wrestled for control of the club behind the scenes, McCoist and Jardine were soon to be the only faces known to supporters.

But starting out life in the Scottish Third Division represented a once-in-a-lifetime opportunity for McCoist to truly put his stamp on the club; to build Glasgow Rangers up from scratch. His team. Two or three experienced faces – the likes of Lee McCulloch, Neil Alexander and Lee Wallace – would surely be joined in the team by a whole host of talented Murray Park kids such as Lewis Macleod and Barrie McKay. There was a long queue of other bright young hopefuls hoping to use the club's fall from grace to further their own ambitions of becoming a regular in the Rangers first team. It was the ideal time to invest in the future.

Ultimately, though, it would be an opportunity lost in the eyes of many followers as the manager preferred to plump his team up with experience while dropping in a little bit of raw talent here and there.

That said, McCoist faced several battles off the field that he would much rather not have, such as the determined scrap to ensure Rangers weren't stripped of their titles by the SPL, who seemed hell-bent on driving the nail as deeply into Rangers' coffin as possible. It was July 2012, and before they would give Rangers the green light to participate in Division Three, they were pressing for more sanctions; quite why, we may never know.

At the time, McCoist said: 'I will not be accepting any talk of stripping titles. That is something we will never concede and everyone at the club shares this view.'

Rangers indicated they were willing to accept a 12-month transfer embargo and £160,000 fine imposed by the Scottish Football Association for apparently bringing the game into disrepute during former owner Craig Whyte's time in control, and that they would also pay outstanding football debts.

One would have thought this, coupled with an unprecedented demotion to the game's bottom tier, might have been punishment enough for the reckless actions of two individuals, but it seemed the powerbrokers of Scottish football were baying for blood, as were supporters of every other club in Scotland.

But McCoist was adamant that stripping the club of titles they had won – which no one in the land could prove were won by anything other than fair means – would never happen, and he was true to his word.

His buzz phrase at the start of The Journey was 'We Don't Do Walking Away', and it was a slogan that really caught the imagination of the Ibrox paying public who, to a man, backed the gaffer throughout the first two seasons in the lower leagues.

It was really only when the climb back to the summit stalled during the first season in the Championship that support for the Ibrox legend wavered, with supporters seemingly split on the dugout qualities of the club's record goalscorer.

But while Ally McCoist might have come up short in his dream to lead Rangers back to the top flight of Scottish football, his contribution, especially off the field, will forever be appreciated by Rangers supporters.

Ally McCoist gives out a positive message

Ally and chief executive Charles Green unveil Blackthorn as the new sponsors

Some advice for flawed Ger Bilel Mohsni

Jim Stewart, Kenny McDowall, Lee McCulloch, Ally and Ian Durrant celebrate title success

No holding back as the gaffer takes part in training with Bilel Mohsni, Lee McCulloch and Richard Foster

Manager of the Month

With midfielder Ian Black

Ally caught up with ex-Ger Michael Mols at a pre-season match in Emmen, Holland

Dugout duties in a match against Albion Rovers

Sharing a joke with Lewis Macleod and the Doc

The message is loud and clear

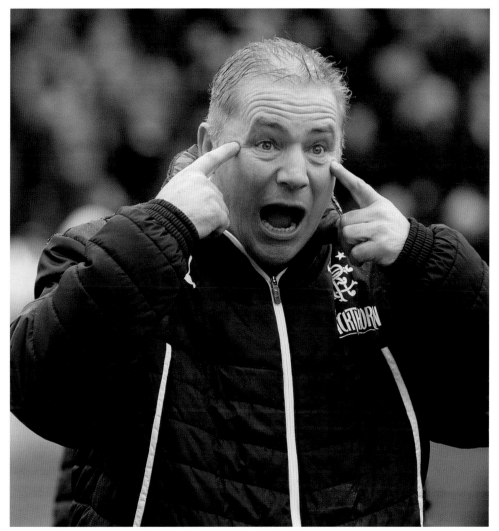

Wakey Wakey!

Ally was a big favourite with the Union Bears

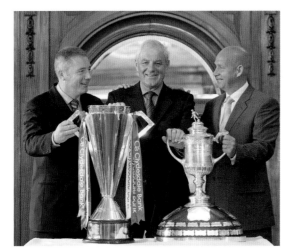

With Walter Smith and Kenny McDowall – and some precious silverware!

A smiling Ally with the League One trophy

McCoist and McDowall cut some shapes!

Super Ally: We Don't Do Walking Away became a well-used phrase on The Journey

The teams emerge under the gaze of Super Ally

A special word of thanks to the young Rangers supporters

Ally has that worried look in his eyes

Alone at the end of the tunnel

Ally has left the building...

Chapter Four

The Supporters

PLAYERS COME and go, as witnessed by the large number used throughout The Journey, but fans are forever – especially Rangers fans.

For many decades, the Light Blue anthem of Follow Follow has been recited passionately on terracings and in stands from Aberdeen to Dumfries, and Barcelona to South Carolina; nothing gets the blue and white juices flowing quite like a group of Bears in full voice.

But the words of Follow Follow were never truer than when Rangers hit their darkest moments in 2012, and the club plunged into administration and then liquidation. While Sandy Jardine and Ally McCoist provided leadership from a high, the foot soldiers rallied round and formed lengthy queues outside the ticket office to buy season books.

This was life after the SPL, Rangers-style, and it was a quite magnificent show of unity, and one which is arguably unparalleled in the history of the Scottish game. But while the rest of Scottish football may have looked on with incredulity, no one within the confines of Ibrox stadium was in the least bit surprised, at least no one with blue blood coursing through their veins, for our supporters are undeniably faithful to a fault.

It reminded me of a trip abroad to see Rangers in the 1979/80 European Cup Winners' Cup. We were in Dusseldorf, and having just seen off Fortuna after a tie-winning 0-0 draw, we were paired with Spanish giants Valencia in the third round. It was a cracking draw, but while neither my mate nor I could afford to go to Spain for the first leg, scheduled for just three weeks later, he made sure he was heading for

the sunshine by pawning his mum's hi-fi unit and video recorder. And while I wouldn't advise any young Rangers fan to take the same course of action, it just showed what it meant to him to follow his team everywhere and anywhere.

Of course, it required a different level of passion to back the team for the 2012/13 campaign. While many thousands of fans continued with their unbroken support of Ally McCoist's side, the unbelievable sight of seeing Rangers frogmarched like a common criminal through the streets of Glasgow, due to the actions of certain individuals, resonated with many more thousands, and persuaded them to return to their club in their desperate hour of need.

With Charles Green on tea duty, staff at the ticket office were overworked as everyone connected with the club flicked two massive fingers at the rest of Scottish football. Those same supporters of away teams who had shared a ground with the Gers' fans were now falling over themselves to ensure Rangers were punished in a proper manner. 'Sporting Integrity' was the buzz phrase as Scottish football went to work with Domestos to cleanse the game of the fallen Ibrox giants.

In their eyes, Rangers had committed a crime so huge they were to be banished to the great football pitch in the sky.

Fine them, deduct points from them, strip them of their titles, we'll sell out grounds without them. Hell hath no fury like a Scottish football supporter scorned. The Scottish game would be better off without Rangers. At that very moment, the vast majority of the Ibrox support vowed never to forgive or forget. The hatred and bitterness towards Rangers sent shockwaves around the world and back.

Now, four years on, we can revisit the land of sporting integrity with the benefit of hindsight and see it exactly for what it was; a sham that had only one purpose, and that was to put the boot into Rangers. I can see no other explanation. Sure, Rangers had to be punished for their indiscretions, but the verdict passed by the kangaroo court was akin to someone receiving the death sentence for stealing a bag of Maltesers out of Asda.

And it was our supporters who bore the brunt of the hatred towards the club. While 'businessman after businessman' arrived in the boardroom in the aftermath of admin and liquidation, promising the earth and delivering zilch, it was the supporters who suffered, with each different suit bringing another stinging right hook to the stomach.

All we craved was stability, and all we got was another spiv. Thankfully, the start of the 2015/16 season finally brought that stability, and Rangers-minded people into the boardroom.

It's difficult to be pragmatic while talking Rangers post-admin. The pain caused by the Craig Whyte-Charles Green-Mike Ashley era is still raw, but surely the Mark Warburton 'revolution' was for the fans, and everything they'd been forced to endure throughout the period which will forever be known, rather kindly, as The Journey.

Mark Warburton gave the supporters back their swagger. The football was exhilarating at times, the players were a step up and the pride had returned to the badge: a badge which had been kissed all too easily in the past. Warburton got the job done quickly and effectively. The supporters who had Follow Followed to friendly soccer outposts such as Elgin, Brechin, Stranraer, Annan and Berwick were suddenly smiling again.

Sure, it might be difficult to get used to sitting in relative comfort at away grounds in the 2016/17 season (instead of balancing on grassy slopes), but for many supporters, visiting the smaller towns in Scotland is something they are happy to have experienced. They've done their time and now they just want to watch Rangers challenging for the major honours again – and that's not too much to ask, is it?

The sun sets outside Ibrox as the first home match of The Journey arrives

And inside the ground...The fightback starts here!

All roads lead to Glebe Park

The Bears arrive in Brechin

Lee McCulloch for the first goal anyone?

Full house at Ibrox for the visit of East Stirling

A young fan chats to mounted police officers as he awaits the arrival of the team bus

Another youngster checks out the latest programmes for sale

The latest line in Morph suits!

Turkeys voting for Christmas!

It's going to be a long journey, Rangers...

Out of the subway. Time for a pint, or straight to the game?

That familiar matchday walk up to the stadium

Kermit at Stenny... for East Stirling v Rangers!

Catering...Annan style!

A hand-knitted Gers fan!

We are the Teddy Bears!

A blue Santa at Montrose

On the terracing at Peterhead

Kermit pops up again...this time at Queen of the South

Captain Carlos Bocanegra says goodbye to supporters

Two generations of fans at Alloa

A muddy marvellous scarf at Alloa

Teaming down at Glebe Park

Brechin plays host to the Italian Lads

Yet another superhero at Ibrox

Loyal to the core, that's Rangers fans!

Rangers supporters are worldwide...

The atmosphere at the Glasgow Cup Final was electric

And a naughty message to Celtic supporters...

A quick peek at the programme at Forfar

A giant Rangers supporter at Annan!

The pies are good at Airdrie...

...and they're delicious at Annan

But they're probably best at Montrose!

Ibrox plumber George runs the Maintenance Loyal

Chapter Five

The Grounds

A SHORT break at a coastal north-east caravan park, or a job in the thriving fishing industry might be the only way many Rangers supporters would ever have ended up in Peterhead. But all roads led to the 'Blue Toon' for the start of Rangers' lower league journey back in August 2012. It was the unlikeliest start to a league campaign in the Ibrox club's chequered history, and a low-key way to begin what was their 140th year in existence.

Driving into Peterhead, you definitely knew the Rangers were in town, as a red, white and blue scarf was tied to the 'Welcome to Peterhead' sign – and Gers flags were all around a roundabout! With a Ramsdens Cup visit to Glebe Park, Brechin, taking place the week before, all the talk of Rangers' demotion had finally become a reality. No more would supporters be served up a regular diet of Parkhead and Pittodrie: for now they would have to make do with dining at the coal face of Scottish soccer. Mind you, for the regulars of Galabank, Links Park and Ochilview, the flip side meant the famous Glasgow Rangers would be coming to town. Interest in the lower leagues rocketed and there wasn't a seat to be had when Scotland's most successful club rolled up at a town near you. Imagine the latest blockbuster movie opening at your local cinema – and multiply the interest and hysteria tenfold when football's answer to Brad and Angelina were in town.

And wherever the Rangers went, the TV cameras were sure to follow. The spotlight had shifted from the much-heralded 'sell-out Saturday' to the only show in town! But if it was an eye opener for Lee McCulloch and co, the same could be said of the Rangers support, who Follow Followed their team throughout the country. They would populate the famous 'hedge' side of the ground at Brechin, marvel at punters sitting in deck chairs on top of garages at Montrose, and check to see if innovative fans were using Dumbarton Castle to get a better view of the action at the Bet Butler Stadium. The anger and resentment at those who had taken great pleasure from our messy demise soon turned to joy and adventure as supporters accepted their fate and embraced the three-year (soon to be four) hiatus. Many of the smaller grounds, with their naturally smaller capacities, were adapted to house more supporters and the general feeling amongst travelling fans was one of great acceptance. Of course there were the taunts from over-exuberant locals, who playfully teased their visitors by suggesting Rangers were a new club. Of course, they were well wide of the mark.

That apart, Rangers made many new friends on the road, and while club treasurers beamed from ear to ear at the beautiful sound of clicking turnstiles, the players more often than not put on a decent show for the paying public – although there were exceptions, believe me!

And of those present at Mosset Park, Forres for the 2012 Scottish Cup tie, who could forget the sight of a tractor pulling a trailer containing several bales of hay along the adjoining A96 road – although it was so close to the ground it appeared the hay was shimmying along the back of the small terracing! There was also a large contingent of fans watching the cup tie from someone's back garden. These were just a couple of the many bizarre sights Rangers supporters would encounter on their journey.

Meanwhile, back at Ibrox, the lively and passionate Union Bears were never slow to show their support for the team, and especially the manager Ally McCoist, who made a point of embracing the BF1 section just a few moments after being presented with the Division Three trophy. There was a feelgood factor – and siege mentality – surrounding games at Ibrox. We were all in it together and no one was capable of destroying that bond. But as we moved up the divisions, and the stadiums became larger, then more supporters could be accommodated. We moved back to playing at semi-familiar grounds such as Stark's Park, Palmerston and Cappielow.

That was probably the moment the Rangers supporters knew it wouldn't be too long before their favourites were getting close to a return to normality, although perhaps very few people around Ibrox knew exactly what normality was anymore!

It's fair to say our first season in the Championship didn't quite go according to plan, and while it was pleasant enough to visit stadiums like Tynecastle and Easter Road again, it would have been far nicer to gain promotion back to the top flight at the first time of asking. That aside, new grounds were visited and many new friends made, although the hope now has to be that the only time we will ever visit

Glasgow Rangers...the only show in town. Even in Sacramento!

the likes of Elgin and Stenhousemuir again is if they somehow gain promotion to the Premier League, or we draw them in the Scottish Cup. Our lower league journey was fun, but it's not something we are in a hurry to repeat. No offence meant, and I'm sure none will be taken!

Not a good night for Rangers in Ventura

Ibrox by night

Now isn't that a boast?

Enjoying the leftovers at Palmerston

An unusual backdrop at Forres

Who needs a ticket at Mosset Park?

'We will need to make that wall taller!'

Watching the game...Montrose style!

Guardians of Links Park...

Welcome to the Scottish League...in England!

Berwick's Shielfield Park is also home to the Berwick Bandits speedway team

Hope mum isn't looking for her bedsheet!

OCHILVIEW BAR

Watch live
football here

Bee-Jay
FLOORING
TEL: 07795 275 422

RESIDENTIAL &
CONTRACT

ALL TYPES OF
FLOORING

WESTWOOD RSC

Rangers fans
at Stenny

Brass band play next to the Highland Toffee factory in Stenhousemuir

Waiting to get inside at Alloa

Measuring the pitch dimensions as Alloa narrow their lines by five yards on each side for the return visit of Rangers to the Indodrill Stadium

Nathan Oduwa performs the 'Rainbow' flick

Elgin's trim Borough Briggs stadium

The scaffolding stand is ready at East Fife

Fans watching the East Fife v Rangers game from a tree

Getting a good view from the temporary stand

But I'm afraid that's the SEVENTH ball they've lost today!

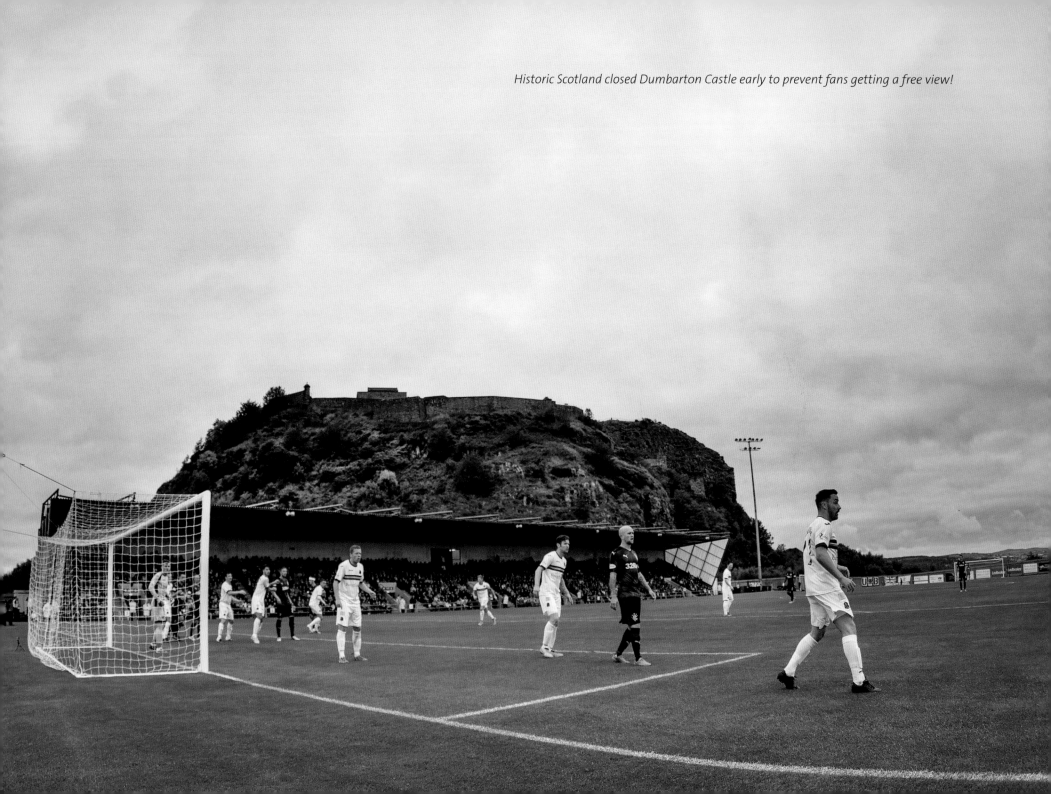

Historic Scotland closed Dumbarton Castle early to prevent fans getting a free view!

A cracking view at Stair Park, Stranraer

Rangers fans start arriving at Cappielow

The stunning Ochil Hills witness an awful game between Alloa and Rangers

Who would be a cameraman – especially at Stenhousemuir!

Rivers of water means no football tonight...

Especially with that wind getting up

Groundstaff work tirelessly to get the Rangers-Hearts match on

Kenny Miller scores against Livi in a snowstorm

Peterhead looks nicer in the summer...

Rangers and Raith players emerge from the tunnel at Stark's Park

The Bears are ready for the action at Links Park, Montrose

Oi, mind the windows!

Stirling Albion and Rangers play under the gaze of the (Lee) Wallace Monument!

Who would like some Forfar fish n chips?

Lee McCulloch leads out Rangers at Forfar

So, just what are you allowed to take in to Station Park, Forfar?

Chapter Six

The Good

THERE HAS been lots to be joyous about over the last four and a bit years, and it wasn't just all about the silverware.

No club does Armed Forces Day like Rangers, and that goes for Remembrance Day as well. Throughout the last few years, Rangers have welcomed members of all Armed Forces to Ibrox to celebrate both the end of the First World War and the Armed Forces themselves.

While one event is poignant and respectful, the other is a bit more of a celebration, and that was certainly the case when Armed Forces Day 2013 took place on the afternoon of the Rangers v Stenhousemuir League One match.

With Rangers 3-0 up at half-time, out marched 400 men and women representing the army, navy and air force. It was a spectacle to behold and, to a man, the large Rangers support – all 43,877 – rose to acclaim the brave servicemen and women.

Anyone present that day couldn't fail to be caught up in the emotional scenes and I will never forget the sight of around 70 or 80 young soldiers doing the 'Bouncy' with the Union Bears, with some even joining the BF1 singing section for the secondhalf! Memories for life, for both those present and the forces personnel themselves. Oh, and Rangers went on to win 8-0, so the extended half-time break certainly didn't do our players any harm.

At the start of the 2013/14 campaign, Rangers supporters were once again proving just how loyal they were by backing the club in large numbers through season ticket purchases. More than 38,000 were sold, which eclipsed – by far – the number sold in many of the previous seasons when Rangers inhabited the world of the Premier League.

Meanwhile, Rangers' under-20s defeated Hearts on penalties to win the Scottish Youth Cup. Young guns such as Andy Murdoch and Calum Gallagher were part of the side that struck gold, proving the future of the Ibrox club was in safe hands.

In fact, there was even a time when Charles Green was popular! It may not have lasted too long, but his gruff Yorkshire personality showed he was well up for a fight with the SFA – which was music to the ears of the Rangers faithful. Mind you, absolutely nothing is for ever!

And another 'bad boy' who was once feted by supporters was French-born Tunisian defender Bilel Mohsni, who was arguably the most unorthodox player seen at Rangers since mercurial winger Ted McMinn.

The man who would eventually leave Rangers for Angers, in the French League, was absolutely everything we wanted him to be – and more – and then he would do something incredibly daft, which had supporters tearing their hair out.

In his first season at the club, he scored a dozen goals and became something of a cult figure. Sadly his time ended when he showed more of a liking for boxing than footie, and his infamous KO of the Motherwell striker Lee Erwin after the play-off defeat to Motherwell.

Despite being down a few leagues, the club still ensured the players would be travelling in style when they commissioned the Rangers 'super bus!'

The coach was described as the best in Scotland after it arrived in the country from Holland. Suppliers Bruce Coaches had invested a significant sum in the bus, which was specially built by Vanhool, and had 41 seats.

The idea was inspired by a trip to look at a similar vehicle in Liverpool, and as well as luxury leather seating with extended legroom, the bus had satellite television, wifi, power sockets, a top-of-the-range sound system and a computer games console.

There were also extensive cooking facilities for first-team chef Paul Lafferty to prepare meals for the squad after matches, and an area for treating injured players.

The management team also had seats with personalised headrests, there were carpets in Rangers' own tartan, and a separate bed compartment which allowed players to rest in privacy.

Sadly, just a month later, the bus was destroyed in an arson attack, which police reported at the time as being premeditated.

Thankfully, there were trophies for the players to celebrate on The Journey, such as the Division Three title. The relief on skipper Lee McCulloch's face when he held aloft the league trophy was palpable, as were the reactions of players such as Fraser Aird, Andy Little and Emilson Cribari.

Equally, when Rangers won League One the following season, it would've taken something pretty special to shift the smile off big Jig's face – as well as his gaffer's!

McCulloch was a massive favourite at Ibrox, cementing his growing reputation by agreeing to remain at the club despite Rangers being demoted to Division Three.

In fact, one wonders if the young fan pictured in this chapter ever did get the Christmas present she craved!

And apart from there being many happy occasions on the lower league journey, it also proved to be educational. I mean who would've thought that supporters travelling to a Division Three match at Montrose would learn all about a famous Norwegian dog?

Bamse – Norwegian for teddy bear – was a lovable St Bernard that became the heroic mascot of the Free Norwegian Forces during the Second World War and a lasting symbol of Norse freedom.

But spare a thought for poor snapper Willie Vass, who, after taking in the Rangers v Queen of the South match at Ibrox, returned to the Albion car park to discover it had been turned into the venue for a drive-in movie theatre – and his car was facing the wrong way!

Without doubt, one of the most impressive performances on The Journey arrived three days after Christmas, 2015, when Hibs arrived at Ibrox hoping to inflict some festive humbug upon an 'ailing' Rangers side.

Prior to the big match, in which just five punters shy of 50,000 packed into Ibrox, Rangers had been on something of a mini wobble, and had won just two of their previous six matches. Some pundits reckoned the Warburton bubble had burst, while others – with a bit more savvy – put it down to a small mid-season slump in form.

Regardless, the home fans were a little anxious in the lead-up to the game, as Hibs manager Alan Stubbs 'talked the talk' in press conferences, while Warburton kept his counsel and insisted his players would do their talking on the park.

And how they did just that. Prior to kick-off, the teams were locked on 41 points apiece at the top of the table.

It was a pulsating game which saw six goals and a red card for Andy Halliday, who later had his punishment rescinded as Hibs midfielder Fraser Fyvie had quite clearly made the most of a nothing challenge to

Glasgow Rangers: The Journey

Ally McCoist with the Armed Forces – as one wag sticks his tongue out for the camera!

get the Rangers midfielder sent off, which sadly referee Bobby Madden fell for.

But Rangers had a definite edge to their play and, roared on by a partisan home support, Jason Holt scored two first-half goals to overturn Hibs' early lead.

Nicky Clark scored on the hour, and just three minutes after Dominic Malonga had cut Rangers' lead to 3-2 late on, Martyn Waghorn scored on 89 minutes to seal the points.

Atmosphere-wise, it was the closest you could get to an Old Firm game, and the vocal backing from the home fans was outstanding.

Hibs simply couldn't cope with Rangers on the day and were lagging behind their hosts when it came to passion and hunger. This was the day Warburton's side came of age – and they didn't look back until the title was done and dusted!

And to 'top' it all off, the last word simply has to go to the guy who made his own magic hat – out of Warburtons bread wrappers. Outstanding, because if you want to get ahead, get a hat!

It's Armed Forces Day at Ibrox

Rangers supporters show their appreciation of the forces

Surely he must score...

*Remembrance Day
card display at Ibrox*

OVER 38,000 SEASON TICKETS
Simply the best sales for years.

Rangers fans showed tremendous loyalty to the club throughout The Journey

Rangers under-20s celebrate their cup win over Hearts

There was a time when even Charles Green was popular...

Makeshift striker Bilel Mohsni celebrates a vital late goal against Albion Rovers in the Scottish Cup

The new Rangers coach

The gaffer is first off the bus

Very clever...first step complete!

Don't dare sit on the gaffer's seat...

A proud Lee McCulloch lifts the Division Three trophy

A young supporter with her Christmas request for Santa (and Lee McCulloch)

Bamse, the heroic Norwegian dog, is a Rangers supporter for the day!

Fancy taking in a movie after the match?

Rangers and Hibs players shake on it before the match

The atmosphere is electric

Barrie McKay skips away from Darren McGregor

The fans have travelled many miles for the match against Hibs

Rob Kiernan is commanding in the air

Jason Holt celebrates his second goal against the Easter Road side

Nicky Clark gets in on the act

Andy Halliday is shown the red card as Fraser Fyvie, right, hangs his head in shame

Martyn Waghorn celebrates his killer fourth goal with Jason Holt and Nicky Clark

Rangers fans celebrate an important victory in the title race

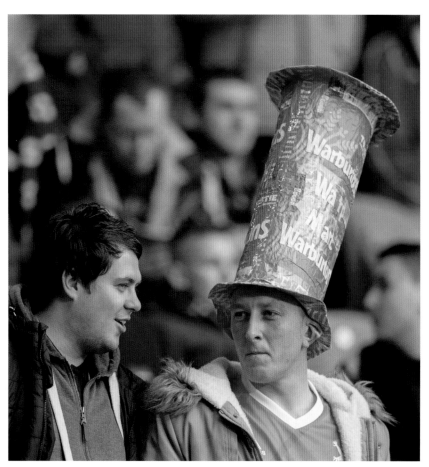

Now, that's what I call a magic hat!

Chapter Seven

The Bad

AS IF going into administration and liquidation, and dropping three divisions wasn't bad enough, there were many occasions during our lower league journey when supporters were forced to dig deep into their red, white and blue resources to make sense of it all.

Perhaps most folk knew it would be a roller coaster ride of emotions, and not just a stroll in the park before making it back to the Premier League. Opposing teams would battle hard against the Light Blues. There would be late challenges and mis-timed tackles, many of which seemed to go unpunished by the lower league referees. For many of the opposition players, though, it was their one shot at glory, and they were determined to take it.

For me, the Scottish Football Association forcing Rangers to wait until the 11th hour before awarding a licence to play football matches was as low as it gets.

It was pathetic, childish, and watching manager Ally McCoist stand on the steps outside Argyll House at Ibrox and thank the authorities for granting the licence made my blood boil. That was the moment my respect for the SFA went completely down the toilet pan. No one should be made to grovel for a football licence, far less a club with 140 years of history, which had proved the saviour for many a Scottish club in *their* hour of need. It was shameful.

On the field, the first two campaigns went relatively smoothly, but season 2014/15 has to arguably be one of the most depressing in the history of the club, with the manner in which the management team and players lifelessly gave in to eventual champions Hearts both maddening and frustrating in equal measures.

After zipping through levels three and four in record time, and with the minimum of fuss, the Championship, while an obvious step up, should have presented little problem to a Rangers team that had been together for two years, but we simply didn't look at all prepared for it, and that was unforgiveable.

Equally, the Ramsdens Cup defeat to Raith Rovers at Easter Road is easily my most frustrating footballing moment – ever. The limp-wristed manner in which Rangers succumbed to the Fife side that Sunday afternoon was unbelievable.

As far as I was concerned, the majority of Rangers players that day weren't fit to wear the famous blue jersey – but that was what we had become. It was the first time I had ever felt that Rangers were actually a lower league club.

Fair play to Raith, but they won the cup with an average side. The sacrifices and commitment made by the Rangers supporters to get to the match that afternoon certainly weren't matched by the players.

The following weekend we lost 3-1 to Dundee United in the Scottish Cup semi-finals. Anyone but them!

Rewinding to season 2012/13, we would remain unbeaten in 36 league matches en route to winning the Second Division, although a pertinent criticism of the management team was that they appeared more interested in going through the season undefeated than blooding hungry new talent in the final weeks of the season, despite the title being in the bag.

Honduran international Arnold Peralta played 24 times for Rangers during that campaign, and looked likely to be a mainstay in the squad for the Championship the following term. The first time I had seen him play, like many fans, was in the pre-season friendly against Newcastle United at Ibrox, and he was like a little tiger, snapping at the heels of his opponents and giving them very little time on the ball. That evening, the Newcastle players certainly didn't relish playing against him.

I thought he could've been a big player for us but he was too often utilised in a more advanced role, when his real qualities appeared to be in a defensive midfield role.

He was eventually released in January 2015, having made just five appearances, including a couple from the bench, and returned to his native Honduras.

Tragically, he was gunned down in December 2015, while out shopping with his wife; a hideous crime that sent shock waves reverberating as far as Glasgow, where supporters laid down scarves and jerseys at the Copland Road gates, and a minute's silence was impeccably observed before the next home game.

We felt the family's pain. It was a senseless crime, and while it may have taken place 5,000 miles away in La Ceiba, the old adage 'once a Ranger, always a Ranger' was never more pertinent…

The message is loud and clear

Ally McCoist on the steps of Argyll House, Ibrox, thanking the SFA for allowing Rangers to play football!

A few Rangers fans hang around to see Hearts get the league trophy

The Ramsdens Cup Final loss to Raith Rovers was a low point

The supporters were in fine form at the Easter Road match

Sadly, too many of the players fell way below the accepted standards of a Ranger

Arnold Peralta was a big part of Rangers' Journey

Tributes to the Honduran international

A minute's silence for the tragic star

Chapter Eight
The Protests

ON THE afternoon of Saturday 28 April 2012, just a couple of months after slipping into administration, a protest march was organised by a group of young Rangers supporters. It was immediately backed by Gers legend, the late Sandy Jardine, who agreed to lead the march from the top of Victoria Road, on the south side of Glasgow, to the front steps at Hampden Park. The aim of the march was for supporters to show solidarity – and their disgust – at the way the Rangers situation had been mishandled by the Scottish Football Association.

As small pockets of supporters began to arrive at the gates to Queen's Park, it soon became clear that early estimates of a few hundred fans would be well wide of the mark. In fact, when the time came to set off for Hampden, more than 8,000 Rangers supporters had formed an orderly queue behind Jardine, and the short walk to Hampden began. The colourful, carnival atmosphere belied the scathing contents of the letter the former Rangers and Scotland defender was about to hand into SFA headquarters.

It was estimated that another seven or eight thousand fans lined the streets to wave and shout encouragement to those taking part in the demonstration.

The mile or so journey to the Hampden steps was good natured, but when supporters arrived at their destination, there was nothing but contempt for those running the game in our country.

Banners saying 'SFA NOT FIT FOR PURPOSE', 'SFA SANCTIONS COST JOBS' and 'SFA KILLING SCOTTISH FOOTBALL' were unfurled by supporters on the steps of the national stadium. And then the crowd fell silent as Jardine addressed them through a megaphone.

He said: 'First of all, on behalf of the club, I would like to say a big thank you to every single one of you. This turnout shows the scale of the injustice served upon our club by the Scottish Football Association.

'And every one of you have proved fantastic ambassadors for Rangers Football Club today. Since the start of the season, when we went into administration, you have turned out in huge numbers at all the games. What you have done for our club has been absolutely magnificent.

'In my hand, I have a letter which I am about to deliver to the SFA, and it says that the punishments heaped upon Rangers Football Club have been unjust. The supporters, players, management and staff did nothing wrong, but if we can stick together and keep this going, then there will always be a Rangers.'

Jardine, a member of Rangers' triumphant European Cup Winners' Cup team of 1972, was given a rapturous ovation, and when the applause died down, he turned and walked into the reception area at Hampden to deliver the letter.

A few months later, he echoed the sentiments of every Rangers fan when he said: 'Taking part in that march was one of the proudest moments of my life.'

Jardine was at the forefront of Rangers' survival fight and quickly became the face supporters could identify with as a succession of charlatans seriously threatened the very existence of our club.

At the time, he said: 'I felt so much for all the workers at Ibrox because they were in a total state of shock after we went into administration, but given the incredible support the club has always had I was always confident we would pull through.

'It really hit home to me that we'd be all right when we marched to Hampden. The idea came from a group of young Rangers fans who arranged a committee on the Friday night and had the whole thing organised by the Saturday.

'To be honest it's one of the proudest moments during my time at Ibrox. To lead that march was a tremendous feeling and I was honoured and privileged.

'There were around 8,000 people taking part and the same number on the street supporting us. I knew afterwards that Rangers would survive. We had to.'

Jardine added: 'I can understand why there was some negative feeling towards the club. Rangers are successful most years, which denies other clubs the chance of silverware. Maybe they have seen this as a chance to get revenge and there's no doubt some were vindictive.

'But even if you don't happen to support Rangers you still have to understand they are a huge part of Scottish football. If you don't have a successful Rangers you don't have a successful Scottish football. Petty jealousies have to be laid aside.

'There's no doubt in my mind the SFA and SPL treated us abysmally. If you look down south at Portsmouth, they went into administration about the same time as Rangers. They were getting help from their FA but I don't think one person from the authorities up here stepped forward to help us.

'To leave us hanging until the day before the season started before giving us a licence and the associated constraints was out of order.'

Jardine helped raise millions of pounds through launching the Rangers Fans Fighting Fund along with Walter Smith. The money was ploughed back into the coffers in an effort to replace the cash that had been wasted by the likes of Craig Whyte during his mis-management of the club.

With Whyte out of the picture, Jardine and co got on with the business of running the club…and then along came Charles Green.

Sadly, Sandy Jardine passed away on 24 April 2014. The Rangers fans had lost a legend; a man known just as much for his integrity and honesty as well as one of the greatest attacking full-backs the club had ever seen.

We mourned the day Sandy passed on, although with the club renaming the Govan Stand in his honour, there is no way we will forget a man who did so much for Rangers Football Club both on and off the park.

Supporters' groups, especially the Union Bears and Blue Order, started to show their feelings over how the club was being run by commissioning a series of hard-hitting banners, vilifying the various people in charge of the club. The banners were massive, and easily viewable from every seat in the stadium – and they got the message across loud and clear. This was a fight that would be taken to the directors' box from those in the stands.

The supporters, mostly in BF1, were incredibly vocal in their condemnation of the board, and some pretty thick skins were required in the padded seats.

Fans' group Sons of Struth came to the fore and upped the ante in the protest stakes. Founder Craig Houston was extremely proactive in trying to force the 'rats' out of the club and their campaign to do so soon caught the imagination of a large section of the Rangers support.

Representatives of Sons of Struth took the fight to the spivs, and defiantly held protest banners up at the back of the Ibrox directors' box, as fans chanted for the directors to vacate the premises.

As the action gathered momentum, protests were arranged outside the front door on Edmiston Drive on matchdays. One that springs instantly to mind is before a Rangers v Hibs evening match, in February 2015, when hundreds of supporters gathered outside chanting 'We Want Our Rangers Back' and other songs. They were joined by

Thousands of Rangers fans prepare to march on Hampden (Picture by Wattie Cheung)

former players John Brown, Nacho Novo and 1980s star, Iain Ferguson.

It was arguably that particular evening in which the pendulum started to swing in favour of the supporters. Crowds inside the stadium were down as fans started voting with their feet, the Three Bears were closing in and it was pretty clear Sons of Struth weren't going away.

Of course, supporters still had different views on how the battle should be fought, although I can't help but think that had Sons of Struth and their supporters not engaged in such an aggressive form of demonstration and protest, we might be sitting here today with the old board still in charge.

Sandy Jardine thanks supporters for attending (Picture by Wattie Cheung)

Rangers legend Sandy Jardine leads the march (Picture by Wattie Cheung)

Rangers supporters are no fans of those who offered little help in their time of need

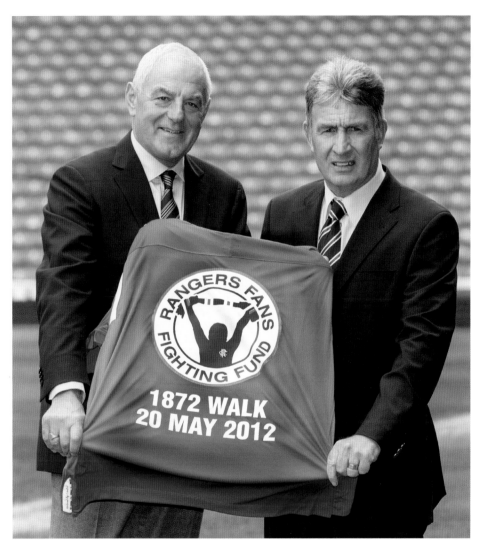

Walter Smith and Sandy Jardine promote the Rangers Fans Fighting Fund

Proceeds from the sales of red and black scarves – the club's traditional colours – went to the fund

Sandy Jardine hoists up the league flag

Former Ranger Colin Jackson's floral tribute to his team-mate

Another member of the Rangers Family taken far too soon

Another classic banner from the Union Bears

Rangers' directors are shown the red card

Sons of Struth step up their protests against the board – in their own back yard!

The call comes to isolate the regime

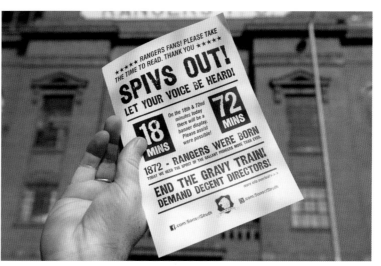

Hundreds of fans took part in a demo against the board before a match against Hibernian

Last call for the spivs...

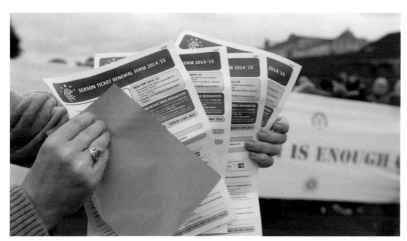

A call from protestors to starve the board of cash

The travelling support at Ayr vent their spleen

Craig Houston from Sons of Struth delivers a hard-hitting message to the club

Rangers fans ahead of the club's EGM

A banner at the Scottish Cup match against Kilmarnock

Supporters protest before the Rangers v Hearts match in 2015

Former players John Brown, Iain Ferguson and Nacho Novo were on the front line

There have also been demonstrations outside the Rangers shop against Mike Ashley

The Rangers fans wanted their club safe from the clutches of the spivs

Rangers fans once again send out a clear message to opposition forces

Chapter Nine
The Play-Offs

AFTER AN opening-day defeat to Hearts in the 2014/15 Championship, successive wins over Falkirk, Dumbarton, Queen of the South and Raith Rovers put Rangers firmly in the mix in the early race for the title. However, home and away draws with struggling Alloa Athletic, and generally dismal form in the lead-up to Christmas, saw Rangers fall way behind Hearts at the top of the table.

The month of March saw a realistic championship challenge crash and burn after four draws on the spin, three of which were at home. Manager Ally McCoist's bubble had burst and the situation at the club was dire.

Protests were rife and supporters were staying away in their thousands. The average home crowd for a league match at this time was around 28,000, but just 14,412 bothered turning up for a Sunday afternoon Scottish Cup fourth round tie against Kilmarnock at Ibrox. The majority of supporters wanted the old board out, and were attempting to cut the cash flow to the club by boycotting matches.

But it was McCoist who quit the club, in December 2014, after a 2-0 defeat to Queen of the South at Palmerston Park. He was replaced by caretaker boss Kenny McDowall, McCoist's assistant, and it wasn't long before McDowall himself was working under increasingly challenging conditions, with the 'low light' obviously being forced to take several loan players from Newcastle United, which he had absolutely no say in. McDowall, clipboard in hand, soon cut much the same miserable figure on the touchline as McCoist had done just weeks beforehand.

But if the football and results in March had been murder for supporters, then April's offerings had all the appeal of a kid playing with a yo-yo. A 2-1 win over champions-elect Hearts was followed by a crushing 3-0 defeat by Queen of the South in Dumfries – a performance which had the travelling support gnashing their teeth.

It was also too much for McDowall, who left the club shortly after the match, paving the way for ex-Gers legend Stuart McCall to join as caretaker boss in a bid to get Rangers through the play-offs and into the Premier League.

It had been a productive few days for the club with Dave King, Paul Murray and John Gilligan finally succeeding in being voted on to the Rangers board at an extraordinary general meeting at Ibrox. That was one positive result for supporters.

With the squad he had inherited from McCoist and McDowall, McCall presided over 11 Championship matches and posted five wins, five draws and just a solitary defeat, away to Queen of the South (who had taken on the mantle of Rangers' bogey team that season).

Supporters had mixed feelings going into the end-of-season play-offs, given Rangers would face the Dumfries club in the opening tie, with the first leg at Palmerston. If Rangers were to go all the way in the play-offs they would have to see off Queens, Hibs and Motherwell.

But they got off to the perfect start in Dumfries, when goals by Steven Smith, from a stunning 44th-minute free kick, and Dean Shiels, with a 75th-minute header, secured a 2-1 victory. In the return match, Derek

Lyle gave Queens the lead – to level the tie at 2-2 – but Lee Wallace scored on the hour to send Rangers through to the semi-finals.

There they met Hibs, who had finished second in the league, and more than 41,000 turned out on a Wednesday night at Ibrox to witness Kenny Miller and Nicky Clark give Rangers a 2-0 first leg advantage. In the return match in the capital, Rangers survived an early onslaught and were comfortable until the dying moments, when Paul Hanlon hit the post and Jason Cummings scored in the fourth minute of injury time – but Rangers were through to the final.

Stuart McCall was set to face the side he had left just a few months beforehand, and whom he had managed for four years, guiding them to successive second place finishes in the Premier League. But on the eve of the match, he insisted: 'It's a strange situation but make no mistake, my aim now is to get Rangers up and having got this far we need to get over the finishing line with one more aggregate win.'

Sadly, the team failed miserably. Whether or not four tough play-off ties had taken their toll, we will never know, but the fact of the matter is Rangers came up short, quite a bit short, actually, losing 6-1 on aggregate to a hungrier Motherwell side.

There's no doubt the flawed play-off system is weighted heavily in favour of the second-bottom Premiership side, who have to play just the one home-and-away tie to preserve their status, but it is what it is.

Would it have been any different had McCall gone into the tie with his own players – rather than McCoist's? We will never know, but nine-in-a-row legend McCall's time was up. He had been in charge for 17 matches and knew himself that failure to reach the top flight had probably scuppered his chances of landing the manager's job on a permanent basis, even though he'd taken on the job with one hand tied behind his back.

The second leg at Fir Park ended in ugly scenes when home striker Lee Erwin taunted Gers' defender Bilel Mohsni, and pushed him in the back – despite his team winning easily – before looking both surprised and horrified as the Tunisian responded with some kung-fu fighting!

We then had the unsightly scenes of Motherwell fans invading the park, making straight for the Rangers end and inviting the away fans on to the park for a fight. Missiles were also thrown at the Rangers fans while it appeared those in authority – the police and stewards – stood back and watched. Despite the strongest provocation possible, the Rangers supporters behaved impeccably.

The entire afternoon at Fir Park had left a bitter taste in the mouth.

Ally McCoist quit Rangers after losing at Queen of the South

A few minutes before kick-off and not many fans heading to the match against St Johnstone

Kenny McDowall had an unhappy spell in charge of the club

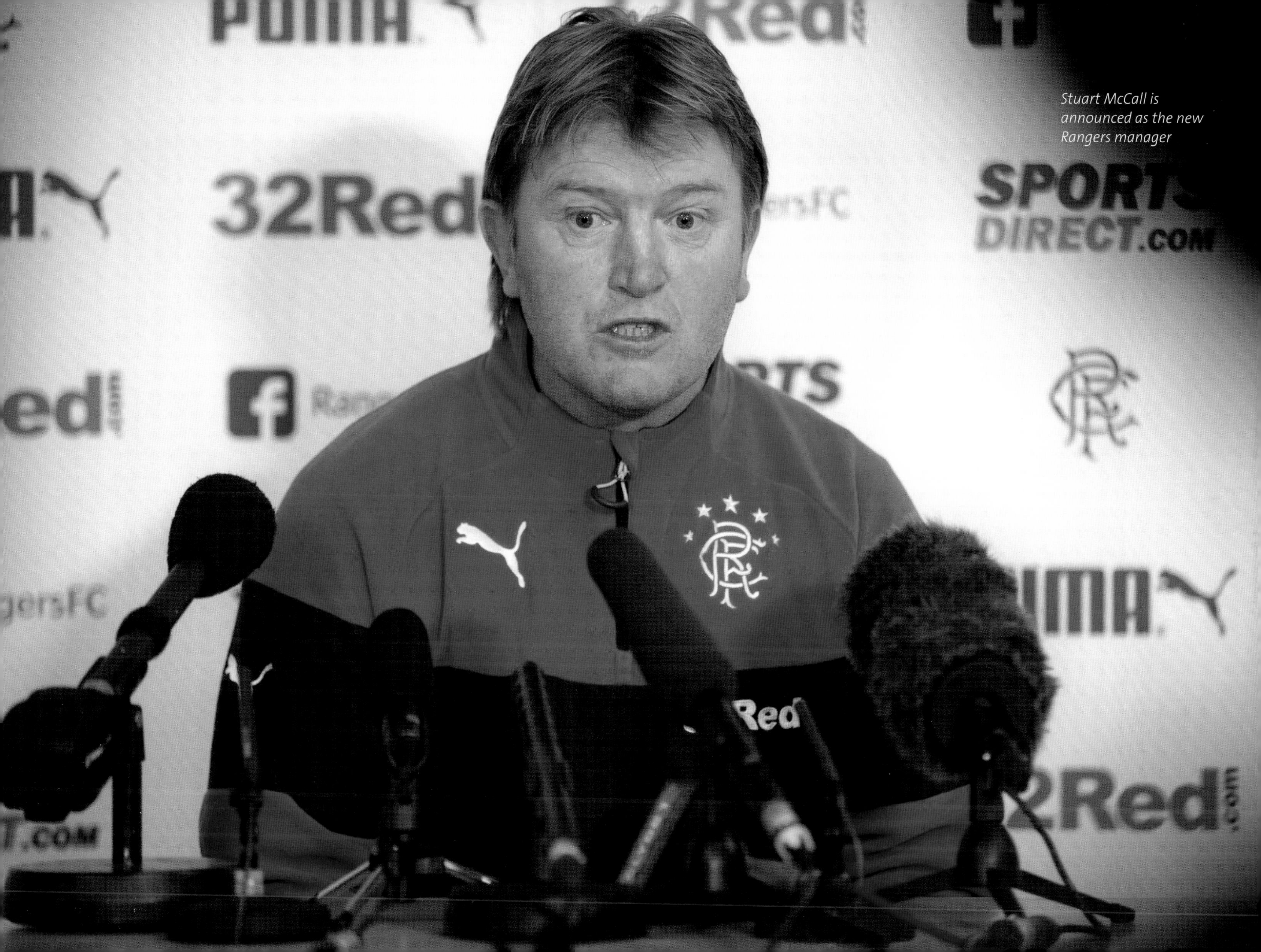

Stuart McCall is announced as the new Rangers manager

And the Three Bears – John Gilligan, Dave King and Paul Murray – have finally gained control of the boardroom

Paul Murray, John Greig and Dave King in the Ibrox trophy room

*Steven Smith scores in the
play-off game against
Queen of the South*

Kenny Miller puts his old side Hibs to the sword

Stuart McCall is a figure of dejection in the play-off final against his former side

Motherwell fans taunt their Ibrox counterparts

Bilel Mohsni lashes out at Motherwell's Lee Erwin

Chapter Ten

The Gaffer #2 – Mark Warburton

LITTLE IF anything was known of Mark Warburton when he arrived at Ibrox to take over the managerial reins. But whereas Ally McCoist had led us into The Journey, and beyond, Warburton certainly finished the job in some style.

In his first ever programme column as the 14th manager of the club, for the friendly match with Burnley, he spoke of it being a 'privilege and honour' to be manager of Rangers, and it was that sort of class and integrity he carried throughout his first season in the hot seat. He also spoke of being 'immediately aware of the history, the stature and the expectation' surrounding Rangers in those same notes. And with that he urged the supporters to exercise a little patience while he built a side capable of taking Rangers back to the Premier League.

Of course, Rangers supporters aren't exactly known for being the most patient and forgiving in the world, but to their credit they bought into Warburton's way of thinking and the players – most of them previously unknown this side of the border – were made to feel nothing but welcome at their new home. And there was patience, generally in abundance, as Warburton stamped his authority on the team almost instantly. Of course, an early 6-2 win over main challengers Hibs at Easter Road helped enormously. It was the perfect way to endear yourself to a new set of supporters.

The results were positive, as were the performances, and long before Christmas Ibrox regulars knew that Mark Warburton did indeed possess a magic hat! Of course, the recruitment of players had been critical,

and that's where Warburton and his assistant, former Rangers favourite David Weir, ably assisted by the head of recruitment, Frank McParland, played a blinder.

Mind you, supporters could've been forgiven for turning to Google to find out a bit more about some of the first wave of players to sign on the dotted line. Waghorn, Kiernan, Foderingham, Tavernier? It was a classic case of 'in the manager we trust', even though trust was something that was rather understandably in short supply at Ibrox, given events of the previous few years.

We all knew about Andy Halliday from his time at Livingston and his upbringing as a bona-fide Rangers supporter. Former Hearts youngster, the talented Jason Holt, arrived in the south side of Glasgow and suddenly Warburton's squad was beginning to take shape. A trio of loan signings from the north of London in the form of Dominic Ball and Nathan Oduwa (Spurs) and Gedion Zelalem (Arsenal) and we were more or less good to go.

Tavernier hit the ground running. For a full-back to score in nine of his first 14 matches was an incredible feat. But it was also testament to the manner in which Warburton and Weir wanted Rangers to play. The team passed the ball around and tormented opposition defenders with the incredible percentage of possession they enjoyed. Patience was indeed a virtue, and there would be no panicked shots or aimless crosses into the box. Warburton had noted that very few goals were yielded from corners lumped into the box, instead preferring his creative players to use their talents to open up defences like a tin of sardines. And it worked more often than not. Rangers scored more goals than any other team in the Championship – both home and away – and while they tailed off a bit at the end of the campaign, the job had been done.

After the final home game of the season, against Alloa in the league, Warburton and his players went on a traditional lap of honour at the final whistle. It was an emotional afternoon and it was no surprise that some of the biggest cheers were reserved for the man who had arrived at Ibrox just ten months beforehand as a virtual unknown, but who, on that afternoon, was the name on everyone's lips.

As the song goes, 'Warburton is magic, he wears a magic hat!' He certainly does, and I'm sure the Rangers supporters, to a man, applaud the vision of an Ibrox board who stuck to their guns and got the man they wanted to lead the club into a new era. It was the best bit of business Rangers Football Club had completed in quite some time.

Mark Warburton and Davie Weir are the new management team

119

The new gaffer takes training

Mark Warburton and Dave King at the Rangers AGM

Early individual success for the gaffer and full-back James Tavernier

Warbs proudly shows off the Championship trophy

And also the Petrofac Cup

Warburton has a special relationship with his captain, Lee Wallace

Jason Holt has been a great signing

The Dream
Team: Davie Weir,
Frank McParland and
Mark Warburton

Chapter Eleven

The Relief

IMAGINE BEING interviewed belatedly by police officers keen to find out what you were up to on a certain date, say, three months or even years beforehand. 'Excuse me sir, but can I ask where you were and what you were doing on the evening of Tuesday 5 April 2016?'

It would be a difficult one for most people, but not if you were a Rangers supporter, because on that night, more than 48,500 of them were packed into Ibrox Stadium for the visit of fellow Championship side Dumbarton.

It was the evening on which victory would assure Premier League football for the 2016/17 season. But this wasn't just any old promotion party; it was potentially the ultimate promotion for a side that had just spent – rightly or wrongly – four years in the lower reaches of the Scottish game.

Victory would secure a precious berth in the top flight, but more importantly it would signal the end of The Journey, a period in the history of Rangers Football Club blighted by awful financial management, shady characters and protests every other week.

Leaving aside the wrecking ball tactics of the football authorities and other clubs – whom previous Rangers sides had bailed out on more occasions than anyone would care to remember – it was a period spent in the doldrums, with many supporters genuinely worrying for their club's future.

Victory over Dumbarton, a team Mark Warburton's men had already beaten three times in the Championship that season, would mean promotion was guaranteed, and it was the least the huge, expectant crowd were demanding.

However, history shows that such occasions are fraught with danger, and that a defeat for the favourites is often the outcome – but all we wanted was to get over the line.

Sure, Rangers weren't at their best that evening but a James Tavernier goal – who else? – was sufficient for the celebrations to begin. From the moment Tav got on the end of a Jason Holt cross to sweep the ball into the net, nothing else mattered.

It was the moment we had all been waiting for. In many ways it was inevitable that Rangers would indeed return to the Premier League, but the failings of the first year in the Championship were always lurking in the subconscious of many supporters.

After the match, David Weir said: 'The players have worked exceptionally hard this season, and the goal has always been clear – to gain promotion, and they've done that with a bit to spare.

'Since Rangers were demoted there have been many lows and disappointments, so it's nice to see that hope back in the fans' eyes and to take the club another step closer to where we want to be.

'To play a small part in that is great for us, but more importantly for the players. It's great for them to have that on their resume, the fact they have got Rangers back into the top flight.'

The 90 minutes against Dumbarton is hardly likely to ever achieve classic status, but in terms of importance, it's up there with the best.

Supporters came from as far afield as Australia to see Rangers clinch promotion back to the top flight

Rangers were suddenly free of lower-league stigma and back where they belonged.

The team on a night of great celebration was Foderingham, Tavernier, Kiernan, Wilson, Wallace, Halliday, Holt, King, Forrester (Shiels), McKay (O'Halloran) and Miller (Clark).

The final score was 1-0, but that was irrelevant (even though we would've liked more), because on this occasion the three points were all that mattered.

The one overriding emotion I sensed at the full-time whistle was relief, while many tears were also shed. The Championship title had been secured, at the second time of asking, and we waved goodbye to the lower leagues.

Sometimes it is simply just time to go, and this was our time.

The Ards Chosen Few were also present

As were the Luxembourg True Blues

The title was always in the bag!

A young Rangers fan beams with delight as his heroes take to the field

A sold-out Ibrox to watch the league champs

Jason Holt challenges Dumbarton's Jamie Lindsay

Michael O'Halloran in action

James Tavernier and Barrie McKay celebrate the only goal of the match

Tavernier with a 'champions' scarf

Rob Kiernan and Harry Forrester celebrate

Billy King, Ryan Hardie and Jordan Thompson on a lap of honour

Andy Halliday takes the acclaim of the Rangers supporters

And he gets up close and personal with the Union Bears

Rob Kiernan's magic hat

The gaffer's lap of honour

Chapter Twelve
The Big Match (two in a row)

Sunday 10 April 2016
Petrofac Cup Final – Rangers 4 Peterhead 0

APART FROM righting a very serious wrong (the fact we hadn't won the Challenge Cup in three attempts), the match against Jim McInally's Peterhead was the perfect opportunity for those in Light Blue who hadn't previously graced Hampden's turf to do so seven days before the Old Firm Scottish Cup semi-final.

Former players spoke of the need for guys like Waghorn, Tavernier and Foderingham to get a feel for the national stadium before the match with Celtic; to walk through the imposing front door, get changed in the dressing room and play on the pitch – the whole package.

Around 46,000 Rangers supporters were inside Hampden to watch the final, and they saw Rangers dominate the opening and closing exchanges, with a sticky patch in the middle. But from the moment Kenny Miller slid a low pass across the goalmouth in the 17th minute, and the ball was knocked home by Peterhead defender Ally Gilchrist, there was only ever going to be one winner.

Peterhead were massive outsiders to win the match at 22/1, and the bookies were spot on.

The playing surface – just five weeks old – was an absolute shambles, and cut up so badly it was like playing on a ploughed field in some parts.

But five minutes before the break, the supporters were treated to a special goal by a special player. James Tavernier scored from roughly 25 yards, and it was a volley with class stamped all over it. It was his 14th of the season, and perhaps the best of the lot.

Late goals by Andy Halliday and Miller set the seal on a comfortable win, and a second trophy in six days – following the clinching of the Championship – was winging its way to the Ibrox trophy room. The supporters celebrated as Lee Wallace was presented with the silverware, and the ticker tape shot into the air. It was a case of one down, one to go!

It was also an example of the improvement Rangers had made in the previous four years. Peterhead had been the first league opponents on The Journey, and had come within a whisker of posting a historic victory. This time, though, there was no chance of a repeat. They were simply swept away.

Sunday 17 April 2016
Scottish Cup semi-final – Rangers 2 Celtic 2 (after extra time – Rangers won 5-4 on penalties)

IT DOESN'T get any bigger than an Old Firm semi-final, especially when Scotland's biggest rivals haven't played one another for around a year, and before that it was three!

Before the game, I was standing outside the front door at Hampden, at the foot of the steps with my son, waiting on a friend, when down from the main reception walks West Brom's James McClean and two growly mates, all with Celtic scarves on, and no doubt having just picked up comps (am I judging?). It was the type of sight that helps get you 'up' for the game, as if you need an added incentive. English football's public enemy number one with a green and white scarf on!

The atmosphere pre-match inside the stadium was phenomenal, although it must be said expectations were perhaps a little higher in the Celtic end than in the blue and white half. Why? Because they had won/ were in the process of winning the Premier League and Rangers were still technically playing Championship football – but that's not to say the most positive of Bears were at Hampden to see anything other than a win for the Magic Hat & Co!

Mind you, after just 16 minutes, when Kenny Miller showed a true poacher's instinct to wheel and fire past Craig Gordon (thanks to an 'assist' from Scott Brown), I started to believe – but desperately wanted the match to end there and then.

But when Celtic equalised five minutes into the second half, I switched back to the negative and thought it wasn't going to be our day, despite the fact Rangers had played by far the better football in the first half, and looked much more like the top league side than Celtic.

Into extra time, and Barrie McKay picks up the ball about 30 yards from goal, flicks it past Scott Brown and arrows a shot beyond the despairing arms of Gordon. A 'once-in-a-lifetime' shot from McKay, according to one pundit, even though the wee winger has stuck quite a few of them in the pokey since!

To be honest, it was a goal fit to win any Old Firm semi, although Tom Rogic scored ten minutes later to take the tie to penalty kicks. It seemed harsh that Rangers, having had 63 per cent of possession, should be taken to the lottery of penalties, although the singing and dancing was all coming from the Rangers end ten or 15 minutes later when Halliday, McKay, Law, Wallace and Zelalem all held their nerve to score – at the Celtic end – and Rogic blasted his ball in the direction of Venus! Although I should mention Wes Foderingham's terrific penalty save – from Scott Brown.

I have been watching Rangers for 45 years and witnessed many a great occasion, both European and domestic, but this was by far the happiest I had ever felt after a game. 'Joy unbridled' I believe they call it. It was all that and more, and I wasn't alone.

As soon as Rogic missed the last penalty, Lee Wallace and co raced to the traditional Rangers end, where one massive party broke out, and it was a party – no doubt for some folk – that would go on for quite some time. The memory of the previous season's tame League Cup semi-final defeat at Hampden was wiped away by a confident and talented group of players.

Rangers had struck right at the very heart of the Premier League. If that was the best they had…

*Petrofac final managers
Mark Warburton and Jim
McInally shake hands*

James Tavernier hits a wonder goal

Andy Halliday scores from the spot

Kenny Miller with the cup – and a magic hat!

A special message from the Union Bears

Harry Forrester and Martyn Waghorn with the cup

Lee Wallace mingles with the club's supporters

Rangers fans do the Bouncy

Kenny Miller delivers a killer blow to Celtic

Celtic's Patrick Roberts misses an open goal

Barrie McKay lets fly – and the ball flashes past the helpless Craig Gordon

Wes Foderingham pulls off a stunning save

Even Mark Warburton can't look

Some of the Rangers players can't bear to watch the penalties

But Wes Foderingham makes a great save from Scott Brown

And it's time for the Gers stars to begin the celebrations

Foderingham is the hero

Joy unbridled at Hampden

Mark Warburton with the Scottish Cup...we can dream!

Chapter Thirteen
The Disappointment

Saturday 21 May 2016
Scottish Cup Final – Rangers 2 Hibs 3

FOLLOWING THE highs of clinching the Championship title and winning the Petrofac Cup – not to forget outplaying, and beating, Celtic in the semi-final – Hibs lay in wait in the Scottish Cup Final. The season's finale and two second-tier clubs were set to battle it out for the country's premier cup competition.

Rather worryingly, Rangers had endured a three-week wait without a competitive fixture prior to the final, as Hibs attempted to battle their way through the Premier League play-offs, a mission they ultimately failed in against Falkirk.

But they at least had a few competitive matches behind them, while Mark Warburton's men had been twiddling their thumbs, training and getting some sun on their backs. It was hardly the ideal preparation for such a big match, but hardly the fault of anyone at Ibrox.

Still, there was a buzz of expectation as an army of supporters clad in red, white and blue clambered up the stairs and into the traditional Rangers end at Hampden, and by the time the teams had made their way out on to the pitch, the Bears were looking forward to the prospect of clinching a unique treble against the Easter Road men.

There had been a fair bit of needle between the sides throughout the campaign, with Hibs boss Alan Stubbs regularly taking the lead when it came to pre-match media hype, while Mark Warburton kept his counsel and preferred to let his players do their talking on the pitch.

However, Anthony Stokes got Hibs off to a flying start when he banged in the opener after just three minutes, although Kenny Miller scored midway through the first half to level matters.

And when Andy Halliday fired home a peach of a shot on 64 minutes, there really only looked like being one winner, but Stokes was afforded time and space to head home with ten minutes remaining. Extra time looked a nailed-on certainty but Hibs scored again in injury time.

The last-minute goal proved to be the winner; there was no time for a dramatic rescue mission, and by the time referee Steven McLean sounded the final whistle, most Bears were already making their way rather despondently to the conga line of waiting cars and supporters' buses.

And then the trouble began. Thugs bedecked in green and white, and masquerading as football supporters, invaded the pitch and a number of Rangers players were assaulted. It was put down to 'over-exuberance' by some folk in authority who really should've known better.

The bottom line was, and still is, that the pitch invasion and subsequent cowardly assaults were the work of hooligans out to cause trouble. Once again, though, the ham-fisted football authorities and media got their post-match post-mortem completely and utterly wrong, with some suggesting Rangers supporters had been equally as culpable as their Edinburgh counterparts. You simply couldn't make it up...

The season might have ended on a low note, but the ultimate mission had been accomplished.

The Blue Order are ready for the cup final...let it begin

Could this be our day?

Not a ticket to be had for love nor money

The players arrive to a giant card display

Andy Halliday scores for Rangers

Kenny Miller celebrates another cup final strike

Martyn Waghorn's cup final strip

Former Ibrox favourites
Nacho Novo and
Jorg Albertz cause a stir
in the Rangers end

Hibs fans invade the pitch
and challenge Rangers
supporters to a fight

The crossbar and posts
disappear in a show of
'over-exuberance' from
Hibs fans

Chapter Fourteen

The Return

IT SEEMS a lifetime ago that Rangers last populated the Premier League. Of course, it has been four seasons; three largely enjoyable ones and a solitary campaign in the Championship to forget.

The close season had been an interesting one, to say the least. Mark Warburton and David Weir knew they had to add to the squad that had got them over the line in the league last season, and won the Petrofac Cup, not to mention a stunning Scottish Cup semi-final success over Celtic.

Josh Windass and Matt Crooks arrived from Accrington Stanley, Matt Gilks as back-up to Wes Foderingham. In came Lee Hodson and Clint Hill to bolster the defence, and Joe Dodoo from Leicester City and Preston's Joe Garner to help Waggy up front. Jordan Rossiter, who arrived from Liverpool, looks a real find in the middle of the park.

And then the big names. Niko Kranjcar. More than 80 caps for Croatia and a midfield ace with previous at Tottenham Hotspur, Portsmouth and Queens Park Rangers. And as if that wasn't enough, Joey Barton signed on the dotted line. Manchester City, Newcastle United, Marseille and a troubled reputation.

The one commodity Rangers seemed to lack last season was a bit of steel in midfield. As good as they were, the likes of Jason Holt, Andy Halliday and Harry Forrester weren't exactly known for letting opposition players 'know they were there'. That was about to change.

So, the first match back in the top flight was one that Rangers supporters had been keenly anticipating since the fixture list was announced, and the match against Hamilton Accies was a sell-out a week or two in advance. Mind you, the game could've been against Dukla Pumpherston and 50,000 Bears would still have rolled up at the stadium. It was all about the Rangers.

'Back by Unpopular Demand' said one banner in the Broomloan Front. That just about summed things up, as Rangers supporters have developed a siege mentality over the last four-and-a-half years. No one likes us we don't care, and fans have learned largely to depend on one another.

The sun was splitting the sky on Saturday morning as hundreds of Rangers supporters prepared to march from Cornwall Street, just off Paisley Road West, to Ibrox Stadium.

It was a lively event which eventually passed along Edmiston Drive, and illustrated exactly what being back in the top league meant to the Bears.

There was a real buzz of excitement in the stadium as kick-off (12.30 for the Sky TV cameras) approached – and with every seat in the house taken, the atmosphere reached a crescendo as the team(s) took to the pitch.

It was also the cue for the Union Bears to unveil their latest banners, and those in the Sandy Jardine Stand to hold up coloured cards for another fantastic display, one which read – GOING FOR 55!

Of course, on this occasion it was just the Rangers players who marched proudly on to the field, ready to watch their chairman, Dave

King, unveil the latest league-winning flag for their sterling efforts in last term's Championship.

Just moments before that, the MC had introduced one of the afternoon's guests of honour, SPFL chief executive, Neil Doncaster, who was roundly booed by just about every supporter in the stadium, and looked perhaps a little uncomfortable – and isolated – standing on the Ibrox pitch ahead of the flag ceremony.

But there was a special cheer reserved for Mr King, who flicked the switch and out came the league flag as if by magic! That was the cue for the Ibrox Roar, and the normally stern King allowed himself a wry smile. All those months of fighting to wrestle the club from the hands of 'non-Rangers' men had been well worth the bother – and this was the proof.

That done, the Hamilton players then took to the field and the gladiators prepared to do battle.

It was a largely frustrating afternoon for the home supporters as their favourites huffed and puffed, especially in front of goal, and despite almost constant pressure, and possession, Hamilton broke up the park and Ali Crawford fired home from inside the box.

It was a real blow and Accies then seemed determined to break up play as much as possible by wasting time and committing an incredible number of both petty and cynical fouls. Referee Don Robertson was a weak match official and let far too much go before belatedly clamping down and booking five visiting players.

Rangers were awarded a free kick for a foul on Andy Halliday and Martyn Waghorn and James Tavernier stood over the ball. It was the former who took the kick and struck the post with the Accies keeper well beaten.

It remained 1-0 for the Accies at the break, and the half-time entertainment saw former Rangers striker Iain Ferguson introduced to the crowd, as well as talented wheelchair tennis star Gordon Reid.

Mark Warburton resisted the temptation to make changes at the break, and instead sent on Harry Forrester and Michael O'Halloran for Kenny Miller and Niko Kranjcar on the hour mark. The move paid almost instant dividends with Forrester sending over the most delightful of crosses for Waghorn to steer home.

That should have been the cue for Rangers to go on and finish off the visitors, but they struggled to press home their superiority and a Michael O'Halloran effort, which hit the post, was the closest they came to grabbing the winner.

And with ten minutes remaining, Waghorn went down in a heap while chasing a through ball and was eventually forced to leave the field with a nasty looking hamstring injury.

With the match finishing all square, Rangers were forced to settle for a solitary point, and the vast majority of supporters went home disappointed. Rather appropriately, the sunshine had disappeared and it was raining by the time the final whistle sounded and supporters started to make their way back to all four corners of the country.

But the bigger picture was the return of Scottish football's most successful team to the country's top league. The Rangers might have been back by unpopular demand, but the sentence was served and normal service has been resumed.

We thank those lower league clubs who opened their hearts and minds and allowed us in. We will never forget, but it's time to bid farewell to Elgin, East Stirling and the rest. The Journey was a lot of fun, but it's time to look forward again.

TODAY IS NOT JUST ANY MATCH DAY
    ITS GOING TO BE EMOTIONAL
4 YRS AGO WE WERE KICKED
BATTERED AND BRUISED INTO THE
3rd DIVISION AND AT ONE POINT
WE SIMPLY DIDN'T KNOW IF OUR
CLUB WOULD SURVIVE.
BUT THROUGH THICK AND THIN
WE HAVE SURVIVED AS A GREAT
FOOTBALL CLUB AND WILL CONTINUE
TO PROSPER AS EVERY RANGERS
FAN ALL OVER THE WORLD IS ALL
PULLING IN THE SAME DIRECTION
AND LONG IT MAY CONTINUE.
LETS GO FOR 55

IN LOVING MEMORY OF MY BROTHER GERRY.

The Union Bears marked Rangers' return to the Premier League with a pre-match march.

(Inset) A notice posted on the Ibrox wall

Rangers are back –
and Going for 55!

The Championship flag is unfurled

Dave King keeps a tight grip on the league trophy

Niko Kranjcar in action

Lee Wallace and Dougie Imrie show their desire to win the ball

Joey Barton picks out another pass

The goal is crystal clear

Joey Barton has a quiet word in the ear of ex-Celt Massimo Donati

Martyn Waghorn gets Rangers' first goal of the new league season

And the Ibrox goal machine celebrates in style

Michael O'Halloran is unlucky to see his shot come back off the post

The match ends all square

The sold-out signs are up again at Ibrox

The Fans' Comments

Jonny Reid

From queuing up for free Irn Bru in the third division, to queuing up for season tickets in the Premiership. From Forfar away on a Monday night in League 1, to THAT game at Hampden. From Kevin Kyle to Niko Kranjcar. We are back, and going for 55.

Marcus McMillan

I have absolutely loved every step of The Journey – from the beginning all the way back to the top, and would say the highlights of us working our way through the leagues are Super Ally starting a great journey and Mark 'Magic Hat' Warburton and Sir David Weir ending it.

George Jamieson

I live in Derbyshire but have often travelled to Ibrox from further south, places like Portsmouth etc after finishing work. I even travelled back from Paris to make the cup games against St Johnstone and Kilmarnock in midweek! I'm a long distance tour driver so miles aren't really a problem for me. I once spent three days travelling all over Europe to get to Ibrox, without much sleep, but that's how much I love my team.

Chris Mayhead

When I was eight years old, my grandfather Sonny Nicol called me to his deathbed and said two things. 'Always remember son, we are the people!' He also said, 'I want you to take my place at Ibrox now.'

It was a promise I kept, but on the day of admin I became very upset and somehow felt we had let him down. But I didn't surrender, no one did. I'm 49 now and have never been prouder to be a Ranger!

Ian Archbold

My mum, dad and Fin went to every home game (only Queen's Park away, due to mum and dad being aulder lol...) and even if they couldn't make the cup games at home, they still paid for their tickets and the money 'supposedly' went to the club. Fin was mascot at the Rangers v Man United Legends game, and we were all very proud. Rangers Then, Rangers Now, Rangers Forever!

Jim and Helen Baillie (The Baillie Loyal)

We were lucky enough to be invited to hospitality by Audi on 18 February 2012. A support in shock with only one topic of conversation – what next?

The door to the suite opened and in came Sandy Jardine. Not trying to hide his distress he quietly acknowledged the situation at the club, spoke of his own personal feelings and asked the guests to try to get behind the team that day.

His parting words were – 'Rangers Football Club will always be Rangers Football Club.'

Less than nine months later he was diagnosed with cancer and sadly never saw us return to our rightful place. RIP Sandy.

Kevin Kyle

Niko Kranjcar

Beba Leitch, Auchinleck

When I first found out we had been demoted to Division 3 I felt more of a sense of relief because I actually thought the club was going to the wall, and at least this would give us a chance to rebuild and return to our rightful place at the top of Scottish football.

I enjoyed the journey to places like Elgin, Forres Mechanics and Peterhead, and while the stick from other fans and the media was sometimes hard to take, we knew that if we stuck together it would all come good in the end.

Although some of the football was dreadful, at least we still had a club to support, which was the main thing. It was disappointing that we had to have two goes at winning the Championship but after the appointment of Mark Warburton and David Weir we started to build a decent side that would get us back to the Premiership.

I've followed Rangers since the late 60s and watching us clinch promotion against Dumbarton was as good a feeling as when Brian Laudrup scored at Tannadice to win nine in a row.

Hopefully the younger Rangers fans never have to go through anything like that again and are watching European football in the future. Onwards to 55.

Steven Barr

The day I knew we had returned to top flight football was a day I will never forget. We went through the leagues one by one and did it the right way.

Then we had the Scottish Cup semi-final against Celtic at a packed Hampden Park. We were serious underdogs and after what had happened the season before against them, we were expected to lose again, but out came Andy Halliday and co – minus Harry Forrester and a few others

– and we gave the Premier League champions the runaround in the sunshine.

Winning on penalties flattered Celtic!

Wilf Marshall

One of the first challenges on The Journey was to make sure our Demi was at the front so she could see the matches which, on most occasions, led to her being photographed by Kirk o'Rourke of Rangers and a certain Willie Vass. Initially, she was just another face in the crowd then latterly a targeted subject.

One of the toughest to stick out was the rearranged game at Elgin the Saturday before Christmas (rearranged due to them originally overselling tickets!). The icy wind was blowing sleet and snow across the pitch into our faces and it was so cold Demi had her scarf up over her nose and woolly hat pulled down so all you could see were her eyes. Don't think I've ever been colder.

The saddest was the loss of the much-travelled badge-filled cap that vanished from under a seat at Tynecastle on the last day of the 'car crash season'. Her own fault for leaving it under the seat but very sad that no one thought to hand it in. Mind you, the blanket coverage of its loss on various social media outlets led to offers of replacement badges from Bears all over the globe – so much so that Demi now has TWO hats to choose from on matchdays. All very humbling.

I've been there every step of the way and it has been memorable. We've visited some lovely places we most likely wouldn't have otherwise and met some great people – mostly being welcomed warmly.

And I managed to complete 'the set', although I've still never seen Rangers at Cliftonhill, as we missed Albion Rovers in the league, and the two cup matches were at neutral venues. I watched Albion play East

Stirling, where I bumped into Willie Henderson, who was there to collect a cheque for his late daughter's foundation.

John McGilp

Rangers fans will surely agree the week beginning 13 February 2012 is the darkest in the club's history, but for my family and I, the week ended with even more devastating news when my father died of a heart attack. My family seem to have Rangers and death intrinsically linked, with my grandfather's death coming shortly after the arrival of Graeme Souness, and my grandmother dying while dad was in Monaco on Champions League duty.

On the night dad died we were at Girvan Juniors' Sportsman's Dinner and the speakers were John Brown and Donald Findlay, ironically in the Catholic church hall, where dad had been chatting to Bomber about a forthcoming charity event. The Girvan night was a great success and we'd made plans to meet up the next day, but 30 minutes after the event, dad was dead.

I carried through the plans for a speakers' afternoon in May 2012 in his memory with Bomber and Mark Hateley the speakers. Given Bomber's part in the battle for our club, it was fitting he was there the night dad died. I cannot speak highly enough of Bomber. In the run-up to the first event he invited my mum and I to Auchenhowie for a tour and handed over two signed tops for auction. I'll never forget the help he gave in organising that first event and what he did for our club. We ran three events and between them, and the collection at dad's funeral, raised £11,000 for charity.

To lose Rangers would've been about far more than losing a club. It would've been akin to losing family, a lifestyle, and tradition that for my family goes back to 1887 when my great, great grandfather and grandmother were married in Govan Parish Church, just as Rangers were moving to the Ibrox area. My dad chose to continue that tradition and I'm thankful he passed it on to me.

My first game was in May, 1984, in which Ian Redford and Davie Cooper scored. I got my first season ticket at the start of the 1987/88 season, seats I still have today.

My first Old Firm game saw three players sent to the dock, and dad and I were at the UEFA Cup Final in Manchester in 2008. We had thousands of memories together through Rangers, so his loss and the impending collapse of the club in the same week was just unthinkable!

Mum and I continued to use the season tickets, something we have done since our demotion to Division Three. We almost didn't renew in the year of the boycott, but the thought of losing our seats in the aftermath of dad's death, as his name was on the seat, won the day.

Quite frankly, the football has been appalling, the personnel on the park questionable and listening to Penny Arcade, which we played at dad's funeral, tear jerking, but it's given me the opportunity to spend quality time with my mum.

Winning the league, Petrofac Cup and getting to the semi-final was like old times, and the feelgood factor under Warburton has been immense.

Competing with and beating Celtic, followed by the statement of intent by the board in signing Joey Barton tells me we are back. Contrast that with the previous season when I left Hampden happy with a 2-0 semi-final defeat to Celtic!

To end positively, since admin and dad's death, my wife Stacy has given birth to two sons, Noah and Coby. On 25 April 2015, at the tender age of two I took Noah to his first game, although he only lasted 28 minutes, but we witnessed a white feather, a so-called sign of an angel,

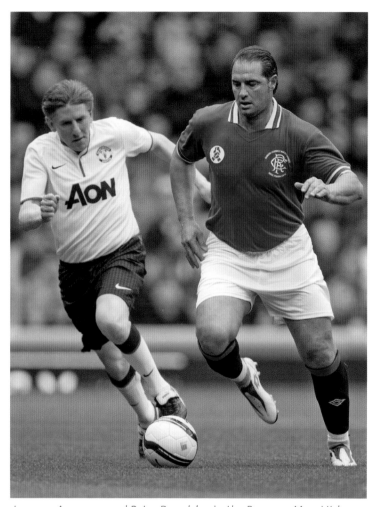

Lorenzo Amoruso and Peter Beardsley in the Rangers-Man Utd legends match

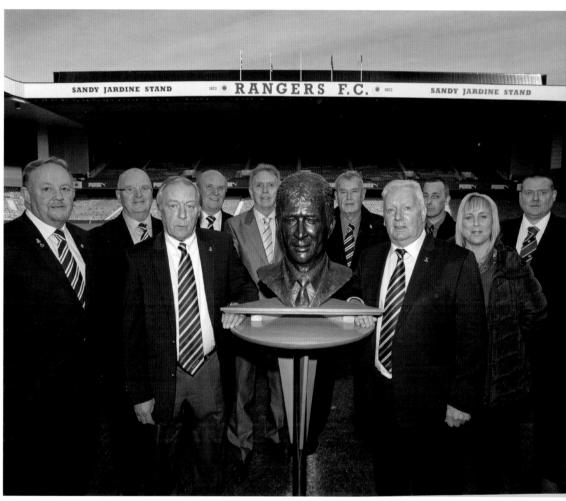

A specially commissioned bust of Sandy Jardine

at the bottom of the passageway to GR1. I like to think dad was with us that day, taking his rightful place with me and my son as he watched Rangers for the first of many times!

Scott Pirie

A 4am start and a long journey ahead. The door goes. It's Stevo with refreshments to accompany the rolls. The bus was on time and packed. The journey was a mixture of dozing off and singing songs and a few hours later we were in Elgin. It was a bit different to the memories of Premiership away days. Instead of being treated like cattle, and marched to the ground, we were made to feel most welcome.

One chap standing outside his pub invited us in. The pints were lined up three deep along the whole bar, the pool table was ready to go and Penny Arcade on the jukebox. A few refreshments later it was time to head to the ground, naturally via the chip shop, which did a great fish supper.

Arriving at Borough Briggs we thought it best to use the facilities before kick-off. This consisted of a wall... no roof, no doors. A step up from some of the top flight grounds to be fair!

We managed to perch ourselves on the grassy hill behind the goal. Quite a windy day, with the odd shower but nothing compared to the frostbite at Stirling Albion that same season.

A pretty uneventful game saw a penalty from Jig and the obligatory red card for Ian Black. 0-1. A lack of action on the pitch didn't lead to a lack of atmosphere in the crowd.

Note: The Bouncy on a wet, grassy hill isn't the best idea for keeping the denims clean.

A wee bit of banter and Andy Walker was left a bit red-faced during TV coverage of the game.

My lasting memories consisted of how well the fans were treated, bouncing about in the rain, a few of us sliding down the hill on our arses and of course that fish supper. About 14 hours door-to-door just goes to show 'Everywhere, Anywhere, We will follow on!'

Alex Boyd

Here are my memories of The Journey:
1. David Murray abandoning us to save himself.
2. Persecution from the Scottish football authorities and the top clubs and their fans.
3. A succession of unscrupulous people milking our ailing club.
4. Unfair treatment of club legend Ally McCoist by some fans who didn't seem to grasp that he was working under impossible conditions from the very beginning of his tenure.
5. Division among the fans.
6. Dave King, who has shown that he is the genuine article by working in the background for the good of the club and not seeking to be on the front page of the newspapers every day.
7. The most awful football matches I have ever seen, even when we were winning.
8. Mark Warburton. No more has to be said, his testimony is shown in the fruit he has bore.
9. Lee McCulloch and Lee Wallace gaining legendary status at the club.
10. WE ARE THE PEOPLE.

Johnny and Andrew Tutin, Aberfoyle Loyal

My son and I have been on this journey together, and what a roller coaster of emotions. Every ground visited along the way, every goal cheered and welcomed warmly in every town. Bill Struth will be smiling down from above, that's for sure. Only a team like Rangers could show the class and dignity that the past four years have given us.

Eddie Green
First game of the Championship season against Hearts, and the renaming of the Govan Stand to the Sandy Jardine Stand, and even though we lost on the day, I was very proud to be on the park flag-bearing with my best mate Davie Speirs.

Gary Havlin (@Rangers Facts)
Like most fans, so many memories of 'The Journey', but the one which sticks out was our first visit to Galabank, home of Annan Athletic.

Stood about ten deep behind the goals for the first half on what can only be described as a concrete block with no gradient like a normal terrace, and all 5ft 2in of me saw absolutely zero of the match, not that there was much to see and enjoy on the park anyway!

Resigned to the fact it was pointless staying in the ground, I left at half-time to head for a pub where hopefully they'd be streaming the game. Outside the ground, directly underneath a scaffold platform, which had been erected for the Rangers TV commentary team, I saw two men wearing headsets and watching monitors in the open boot of their car. It was the Rangers TV production team, complete with monitors and mixing desk, running the live broadcast of the game.

I watched the second half from the pavement outside Galabank, listening to the producer cueing in different cameras and replays and talking to commentator Tom Miller.

Watching the guys at work was more interesting than the football itself! Needless to say, for every away match during the rest of The Journey, I ensured I was in the ground at least an hour before kick-off

so that I never had to watch a match from the back of the Rangers TV production car again.

Ronny Davies
I work most Saturdays so don't get to many games, but I'll never forget our first home match against East Fife. It was the fixture we thought might never happen.

Anticipation is an over-used emotion by football fans, but more than 30,000 fans had absolutely no clue what was going to happen, or what team would appear, as only days beforehand Ally McCoist (the man who stood firm and tall when others walked, no, ran, for cover) had just three players at his disposal.

So, how could this hastily-assembled Rangers squad play Rangers-type football? How many loyal fans disenfranchised by seemingly endless punishments from the SFA and SPL would turn out? Had the Rangers fan base been damaged by these events?

The answer was a firm and resounding no. The Fans, our lifeblood, turned out in force. The game was at best a bounce match, with strange new names on the field wearing numbers 1 to 11, which, in itself, made it seem like a friendly.

I went with my cousin, Davie Wallace, and we took our seats with the look of car-crash victims, haunted by worry, yet strengthened by survival. Every man around us looked the same.

The golden moment arrived when we realised the large number of children present, and how this alone would ensure the club would never die. We welcomed the challenge, Rangers would regenerate into the task ahead.

We won the match, but the important thing that day was who was in the stands.

An impressive collection of badges

Rangers legend John 'Bomber' Brown

Elgin's treacherous grassy slope

Rangers TV covering a game at Annan

The renamed Sandy Jardine Stand

The journey continued, we lost loved ones on the way; the great Sandy Jardine for one, although I'm sure Sandy would be proud of where we are now.

George Fletcher, Okpo Loyal South Korea

Many of the unsung heroes of The Journey are those who give their time and effort to running supporters' buses. They are all heroes in my mind, unpaid and dedicated to the Rangers. Can I say a big thank you to Kevin Niven, who runs the Granite City Rangers Supporters' Club. They have run a bus to all the games in the last four years, which is a fantastic commitment to the cause.

Evan Cunningham

I remember spending all my Christmas money on a day out supporting Rangers in Leith. Full of optimism that Kenny McDowall might actually improve the team. Pumped 4-0. But at least we're in the Premier League now, unlike that bunch.

Jordan Donaldson

Story about my friend Luca and I from last year's game at Ibrox v Cowdenbeath. It was one of the coldest games I think I've been to. We were wrapped up with our hoods shut just enough to see out of, scarves round our faces and arms inside our jackets. With the score at 0-0 and not looking like changing anytime soon, as well as the insane cold, Luca said, 'If we haven't scored by the 70th minute I'm going home. It's too cold.' About two minutes later, in the 60th minute, Dean Shiels netted one into the bottom corner. I turned to Luca and saw the look of absolute despair at the thought of another 30 minutes of minus degrees weather and rotten football!

Alan Marshall

I've been to most away games in the last four years and would say it's been an interesting period to put it lightly. I would say falling in the mud behind the goal at Alloa when we lost 3-2 was a low point. I've got a great picture of me and my pal watching the Stenhousemuir game away in the Ramsdens semi-final from a disabled car park space as this was the best view possible. Some things you just don't forget!

Ben McDonald

One story that comes to mind is the final year of The Journey and perhaps the game that told us it was all but over. Sunday 17 April 2016. Four long years we had been waiting for this. We'd been up and down the country, kicked by footballing associations and beaten by teams I had never even heard of until we were demoted in 2012. Yet the day was here, the day we could beat Celtic and finally say 'aye, we're back'.

For this game, Lee (my older brother) was in the South stand and Grampa and I in the North stand, virtually a stone's throw from the Celtic support. To make things better, my Dad had come up from Jersey, only knowing he had a ticket on the morning of the game.

I'd never seen Grampa so excited before a game, no nerves, just totally confident we would win. As we approached the ground, our support was in full voice, and the supporters' bus rocking as we did the bouncy on the approach to Hampden – giving the odd 'gesture' to Celtic-supporting pubs.

Traffic was at a standstill, and when we got off the bus, Grampa, Lee, Dad and I posed for a rare photo with one another before shaking hands and leaving without another word.

Grampa and I entered the stadium and the nerves started to kick in. 'What if we lose?' 'I canny handle them beating us,' we worried. Taking

It's not always glamorous being a Rangers fan!

Or playing for the club either...

The fans' impressive banner at the Scottish Cup semi-final against Celtic

our seats, we joined in with the songs. Kick-off approached, the teams emerged from the tunnel and I turned to the West stand. It was a sea of red, white and blue. A banner was unveiled – 'We belong to Glasgow'. And Glasgow belongs to us I thought – get right into this mob Rangers!

We all know the result, and the scenes after Kenny's goal were unreal. We dominated from the start, on the park and in the stands. Young Barrie McKay cemented his place as a Rangers star with one of the finest strikes I've ever seen, which even left Grampa speechless!

Celtic scraped penalties, but our lads would stand tall, even when young Gedion Zelalem stepped up to take his penalty. Some fans were scared, but he stuck it away like a seasoned pro, even shushing the Celtic support. How bold!

Rogic then stepped up. Rangers fans sang their hearts out as he took his run-up, and as he struck the ball the stadium fell silent. Over the bar. Rangers had won. What followed next was insanity. I turned to Grampa, in what felt like slow motion, as the euphoric celebrations began. We hugged, jumped and threw ourselves about. Before he let me go, with tears in his eyes he said, 'We've finished The Journey son, we've beaten them, I never thought I'd ever see this again after the last few years.'

As I seen my Grampa, a man who rarely expresses emotion, reduced to tears, I felt a lump in my throat. I realised how much we had been through, as a support and as a family. As the Rangers fans sang and basked in what is perhaps one of our greatest ever victories, Lee Wallace and Andy Halliday approached where we were sitting. These two men knew how much it meant.

Wallace who sacrificed everything for this club and Halliday, a boyhood fan. Seeing how much it meant to Grampa and these players and supporters, I'm not ashamed to say I shed many a tear. Four years of toil in the lower leagues, but it was over. We were back.

Richard Holmes

Travelling all the way to Elgin and falling asleep in a portaloo and waking up at full-time!

Jacqueline Barclay

This is what The Journey meant to my fiancé Darren McRobbie and I. Darren was just a Belfast bloke living his life and I was just a 'Weegie' lass living mine in Glasgow, totally unaware of each other's existence and having one thing in common – we both supported Rangers.

At that time, along with many others, we joined Twitter to get the latest updates on what was going on at our club, as waiting on news bulletins was agonising. It resulted in hundreds of Rangers fans following each other on Twitter for news, updates, support and of course banter!

The months went by and you obviously have more of a rapport with some than others and go on to develop online friendships, which then went beyond football and spilled into the ups and downs of ordinary life.

What started off as chatting about Rangers, then led to friendship, which then led to love – before we had even met in person. Yes, it can happen!

We met in March 2013 in Glasgow and I moved over to Belfast in the April originally for four days. I stayed with Darren for a year!

We moved back to Glasgow in 2014 and now we are both preparing for our wedding next month.

If what happened to Rangers hadn't happened, we would never have joined Twitter or followed hundreds of other supporters, or found each other.

Yes, the Rangers Journey has been a roller coaster of emotions for everyone involved, but I am glad it happened, as I'd never have found my future husband otherwise.

Holly Jade

When we were sent down to the Third Division my dad and I decided we couldn't miss a game. We knew that bums on seats were much needed by Rangers. This we did and I can honestly say I have never been more grateful as along the way we met some wonderful people.

My dad passed away recently and though for some those lower league days were the worst, for me they proved to be the most special time with my dad. I miss him so much.

David Gilmour

Ball stuck in the hedge at Brechin in Division Three – first game of The Journey.

I leave the stadium and start chapping doors for a loan of a ladder.

Finally get one, which I carry round the back of the hedge – but the ladder is too short.

I head back and pay a guy £20 to climb up the inside and get the ball.

He gets the ball, climbs down, puts it in my hands – and a police officer grabs the ball.

I'm told the ball is the property of the club, so I follow the copper back to the main stand where I watch him roll it in among the other balls, making it impossible to identify the original ball.

He walked away laughing – I wasn't!

Chester Parry

I know this is immature, but when you've been unsuccessful in the ballot for the biggest game in four years with BOTH season tickets, and attended every cup game, it can be very frustrating.

I tried everything I knew to get a ticket for the Hampden semi against Celtic but was getting nowhere, so I put a back-up plan in place. The

Jacqueline and Darren met online after Rangers were sent on a lower league journey!

Every cloud has a silver lining, as they say, and Rangers seem to have found theirs.

I know I have found mine!

preparations involved numerous 'props' including doctored emails from SFA employees and a clipboard.

The morning started like any other Old Firm morning, except this time I was ironing a shirt, tie and trousers instead of the usual jeans and polo. Walking towards the station, I heard the sweet sound of some 'tunes' coming from a random house, which put a smile on my face.

The nerves were getting the better of me so I had a wee half bottle to counter them. Anyway, it was too late to backtrack. Initially my plan had been to blag my way into hospitality, and to do so a graphic designer pal had drafted up a mock email from the SFA.

It read something like:

Hi Chester,

As discussed, please attend the Lomond suite around 10.30am on the day of the game and I will send ***** or ***** up to collect you. If you've any problems getting in just show the stewards this email or call me on 07123456789

Many thanks, SFA Employee.

I carried this in a leather-bound folder along with other bits and pieces. Anything to make me look legit. I passed the first security check no bother, but bottled out of the second. God knows why. I sell advertising for a national newspaper so I showed the security man my work's pass and asked where the press entrance was.

'Just at the side of the main entrance,' said he.

'Jackpot, I'm in.'

Jackpot turned to 'shit' when I spotted two stewards standing behind a table, with a box of named envelopes. I look nothing like a football writer, but by this time I was committed.

I showed the guy my pass and he starts digging through the envelopes trying to match my name with one. 'Nope, canny find you here.'

It was all or nothing… 'Is such and such in yet?' I mentioned a name I thought would be in the press area.

'Aye, he's in, come round and we'll find him.' So I followed him round and I'm thinking, 'If this guy is here, not only will I get papped out, but I'll no have my work to go to on Tuesday!'

We sauntered round to the media area and I dipped my head so I wouldn't be spotted. I told the steward I had to nip to the toilet, and that I'd catch up with him. To my surprise he didn't seem too bothered.

After ten minutes, I popped my head round the door and joined the back of a small group of folk who were heading through a set of doors. Where did I end up? The concourse at the Rangers end of the South Stand.

I was near enough right under the police control room and was in two minds whether to jump the wee barrier and disappear into the West Stand. For whatever reason I stayed where I was, looking back up the stairs to make sure there was no angry-looking stewards coming to huckle me.

What a day; genuinely one of the best of my life following Rangers. Up there with Manchester, and as I'm reading this back, I can't believe I saw the match!

Nicola Collison

I'm 40 now and have been going to the games as long as I can remember, and have had my season ticket for over 20 years now.

The day before we went into administration we played Dundee United in the Scottish Cup. Sadly we lost, but a proud and memorable moment was seeing my young cousin Jake out on the pitch at half-time warming up for United. Usually he'd be in the stand with me as he had been from a young age.

The next day and the days after were dark days for us. When we went down the divisions I asked Jake if he still wanted to renew his season ticket. His reply was a resounding yes, as it was important to support your team through good times and bad.

Now four years later we still have our seats along with my young nephew. We're excited to see the good times return to Ibrox and see our team back where we belong.

As for Jake, he's still with Dundee United and hopefully one day he will sign his first professional contract. But I hope to see him grace the field at Ibrox again, although this time in the blue of Rangers. Until that day we continue to support our team from the stands.

Mark Harper, Forres

To have the love of my life come to my wee town in the North East of Scotland meant so much to me. Lots of people asked where my allegiances would lie but there was no question, Rangers, always.

On the morning of the Scottish Cup tie, Forres was buzzing. Members of the Forres Loyal gathered early, ready to deck our two usual haunts out in red, white and blue. First up was the Victoria Hotel. We went into two separate bedrooms and tied our 15ft x 6ft Forres Loyal flag from exterior windows. As the hotel is at a roundabout, Bears arriving in the town would get a nice welcome.

Then it was up to the Eagle Bar, where my mum is the manager – so we decorated it from top to bottom in the colours – and I was in charge of music! An hour before kick-off, it was buzzing, with Glaswegian accents aplenty. There were also boys from the local army barracks, and folk over from Norn Iron.

The game itself was poor, but to have the team I've travelled down the A9 every week to see on my own doorstop was special and something I'll

The afternoon at Forres was a special occasion for one supporter...

never forget. I just wish my granny – who was the most diehard Rangers fan I knew and the reason I am a bluenose today – was there to see it, as it was played on her birthday too.

I will never forget the day Rangers came to old Forres town.

Mark Dingwall

The football licence was granted just two days before the first match (at Brechin). The unholy campaign to kill off Rangers by opposition fans, bent directors and incompetent football authorities had failed. After months of worry and struggle, the football would begin again.

Travelling to the game with old pals we were as high as kites. The pure joy of loving the club flowed – the politics, the hate, the fear – all gone. Only that buzz true football fans can experience – like those first games with your dad or the first away game with schoolmates.

Jig and Ally were guests of honour at a supporters' club function

From our spot on the famous Hedge side we cheered our heroes, guzzled pies, tried to guess the height of the aforesaid topiary, laughed at 'Beefy Stewart' sponsoring a player. Those simple pleasures that come with a day out at the football.

The darkest days were past; sure, we would face more struggles. The score? Who cared? Rangers had survived. The Journey had begun.

Linda (Louby) Smith, Cairneyhill, Fife

My favourite memory from The Journey was being on the pitch with my great-niece Mackenzie as flag bearers on 4 May 2013, when we were presented with the Scottish Third Division trophy in front of 50,048 fans after the game against Berwick.

I felt so very proud of what the team and management had achieved, given all the turmoil we had gone through to get there throughout the season, and since February 2012. I was honoured to be part of the celebrations on the pitch, but at one point I had tears in my eyes as it was such an emotional experience.

Having followed Rangers for over 46 years it's great to see us back where we belong. Bring on 55...

Stan Murdoch, Blues Brothers RSC, Rosevale Bar, Partick

So many memories to choose from.

From the off, when we were hoodwinked into believing our Great Institution was being saved from David Murray's latter mis-management, that we were getting a fantastic consortium of wealthy British investors and foreign friends to help them. Then the unbelievable roller coaster of emotions and financial rape of our great club was at times so painful. But to those who kicked us and tried to finish us off – it will never be forgiven or forgotten!

Thankfully the Three Bears, Dave King, Paul Murray and John Gilligan, and Mark Warburton and David Weir, have calmed the stormy waters and got us travelling in the right direction again.

We set out for Brechin for that first game with a makeshift team, with little backing from an association who had relied on our team and fans to feed Scottish football for years. Spiderman climbed the floodlight at the hedge with the shoe held high. Surreal.

On to Elgin and our bus broke down in Aberlour. Of the 48 on the coach, 36 were transferred to other supporters' clubs buses, while we remained with our driver. The hospitality of the Aberlour Hotel helped as we didn't get back to Partick until 3.15am!

Annan away. Smoochies Bar. Me walking in and saying, 'Hey guys, listen, they are playing Bobby Parks' CD,' before looking round and seeing the man himself sitting at the organ!

Every town and village welcomed us with open arms, and we had many a laugh while seeing places we never even knew existed – in our own country.

Our end-of-season dance 2012/13 was unbelievable, and god knows how I pulled it off – and kept the secret. A chance email request and a bit of toing and froing and we had our captain and manager in attendance. The expressions on the faces of our members when Ally McCoist and Lee McCulloch walked in will go with me to my grave!

And when the Three Bears took over our club, Mr Gilligan kept his promise to speak at one of our charity events, and received the most incredible welcome possible. To round things off, the appointment of Mark Warburton and David Weir was phenomenal, and we achieved our most significant and greatest result of the past four years against our biggest rivals, while the Tavernier goal against Dumbarton that sealed our return to the top flight, had grown men shedding tears of joy.

Scott McClure

At the base of the mountain you can't always see the summit, but when we were sent lower than we had ever been before I knew that one day we would hit the top again, and I was determined to be there. I had an accident, cutting my hand off on 13 March, but still made the next home game. I took my girlfriend to numerous games and even used the notice board to propose on Boxing Day 2013 – a poor 1-1 draw with Stranraer, but Emma said yes and is now my wife. I stood at Hampden watching our semi-final win over Celtic, totally blown away by how far we had come – we all saw the summit that day and when we reach 55 we will have arrived. A journey I will never regret being part of.

Don McLean, Georgia, USA

I have been a fair weather Rangers fan for a few years now, due to emigrating, but even though I kept up with news, scores and transfers, nothing prepared me for the day we entered administration. I'm sure I'm not alone when I say we didn't see it coming.

But for me, that's now history and my personal attitude as a supporter has changed permanently, and for the better. And I see it in the words of other fans. Gone are the days where our focus was on the manager, the coach and the players. We've now broadened our interests to include those in the background. The board are front and centre. We even know their names. We evaluate their decisions, worry and fret over our club's finances, celebrate each new legal milestone and care about preserving our long history. We want to know how much the cleaners are being paid, and if maintenance to the stadium is planned and allowed for. We're simply more involved.

We have all had to re-evaluate our support, and thankfully it has been a largely positive exercise. I for one will be purchasing the Rangers TV subscription (a snip at $299 for the season). I'll be making the pilgrimage to Ibrox with my son, who will hopefully come away with Rangers pride running through his veins like I did in the late 60s. I'll be purchasing new Rangers tops for us every season when one of our last legal hurdles has been breached and I see the club is fully benefiting from this revenue source. And I will continue participating in the discussions, reading the comments and practising my amateur evaluations of players, just like we've always done, even without the internet.

It's simply time to be a full Rangers fan for me again, with all the pride and honour that goes along with it.

Craig Martin, Broxburn RSC (committee)

Season ticket holder since 1988, and have missed less than 15 matches home and away.

It was the weekend of my 40th birthday. I hadn't missed a game that season and my wife said, 'I think we should go away somewhere as a family for your special birthday. Anywhere you fancy?'

Without hesitation, I said 'Elgin.' She soon twigged.

She agreed and we booked into the Premier Inn for Friday and Saturday night and started the search for tickets.

I knew I would probably get one, but could I secure any for my two boys, especially my then eight-year-old, who'd been to many games, and my six-year-old, who was starting to show an interest?

My wife? She could go shopping.

Sure enough, we got two and I tried everything to get more – tweeting players, writing to the ticket office, speaking to a contact in the press – but nothing. Then, on the week of the match, a limited number of additional tickets became available for supporters' clubs. I managed to get one, and was delighted.

I had just checked into the hotel when my mate called. 'Have you heard the news? The game's off!'

He said the police had cancelled because Elgin had sold too many tickets. 'Yeah right,' I replied.

He finally convinced me he was telling the truth. I was gutted. What were we going to do all weekend in Elgin?

We went for dinner and a few drinks and went to bed. On the Saturday morning, we took a trip to Borough Briggs. Sky were dismantling their set-up – studio box, cabling – so we nipped into the ground through one of the exits. 'Are we allowed in here?' asked one of my boys.

'I don't care,' I said. 'I've got a ticket!' We took some photos and left.

The rest of the weekend we went swimming, go-karting and ate some nice food. It was a good birthday, but watching Rangers would have topped it off!

Greg Jamieson

Willie Vass happened to catch me and my dad sat slumped behind Ally McCoist in the Stirling end during the Stirling Albion v Rangers game in October 2012.

I'm sat with my hand on my face and dad is to the left of me with his glasses on.

Stirling Albion were dubbed 'the worst team in Britain' and ended up winning the match 1-0. After exhausting all efforts to buy tickets at the game myself and my dad made a daring entrance through a side door to get in at half-time. During our efforts we saw one supporter watching the game from a tall wall, a police officer told him to get down to which he responded, 'A canny am stuck.'

We spotted another boy watching the game from high up on a tree. He was told to get down by the police, to which he responded, 'Naw!'

The seat we ended up in was the one Kyle Hutton must have used in the first half, because he came out after the interval and discovered we were sitting in it. I got a picture with him and he headed to the dugout.

We had made various attempts to get into the ground before eventually doing so and were relieved to be there. The result was awful, but it's fun to look back on.

We had beers in a lively Stirling city centre before and after the game. All in all it was a memorable occasion, an odd one, but indicative of the early/hazy days of The Journey.

John McQueen

No Rangers supporter will ever forget 2012, least of all myself, as it was also the year I got married!

As I proposed to Margaret it would have been impossible to predict the turmoil about to develop at Ibrox. As people, we all know we will die one day, but we think our football club will survive long after we're gone.

Suddenly, we were facing the unthinkable: that Rangers Football Club was about to die. Fortunately it didn't happen, but it was close and from 14 February to that first Ramsdens Cup game against Brechin, we were all staring into the abyss.

Rangers had been downsizing for a few years, yet still managed to win three SPL titles under Walter Smith, who was generally considered to have saved the club from going bankrupt with those titles and subsequent Champions League qualifications. We had watched star player after star player leave, yet when Craig Whyte took over in 2011, it seemed to be the start of a new era.

It was anything but, though, and around Christmas it all started to go wrong. Celtic overturned our huge lead and Nikica Jelavic was sold. And no Rangers supporter will ever forget where they were when the news came through that we had entered administration. I was informed by a jubilant Celtic fan when I came back from my lunch at work. I will never forget that sick feeling in my stomach. Though it is a ridiculous comparison to make, it did feel a bit like being told a family member had become seriously ill.

The next four months saw us lurch from one false hope to another. However, I had a big distraction – my impending July wedding. Getting married is stressful in itself, but with both events coinciding, they cancelled each other out.

It was painful seeing Rangers endure ten-point deductions, players leaving, being booted into Division Three, out of Europe and then the threat of not being allowed to play football at all. And then I saw the 'breaking' yellow news feed on Sky Sports News reporting that HMRC had rejected the CVA – a week before my wedding. It seemed any kids we ever had would not be going to see Rangers with me, as there would be none to go to.

Guys like my dad refused to believe what was going on. Rangers and our fans had funded Scottish football for over a century – surely somebody would do something to help. But he had his eyes opened that spring. Internet bigots could do more damage than any on the terracing, and the sickening hatred towards Rangers manifested itself like never before. Boards at other SPL clubs gave in to their vitriolic fans and plunged the dagger in deeper.

Back in wedding mode, I had lots of things to do, like write my groom's speech. Did you know that the ancient Mayan civilisation predicted the world would end in 2012? I didn't know they were Rangers fans too!

But we received a warm welcome from the lower league SFL sides – and at least they appreciated the financial benefits we would bring, and most of their supporters had no grudge to bear. At that level, many/most supporters support both their local team and the 'big' team, which in most wee towns continued to be Rangers.

As I jetted off on honeymoon to the Greek island of Zakynthos, at least there was some hope. This new set of footballing circumstances could be viewed as a novelty, a new experience, only to be endured for three years, and probably shorter as no doubt greedy senior clubs would vote in some kind of league reconstruction before then.

When I asked the barman in one of the pubs on the strip in Kalamaki if they would be showing Brechin City v Rangers, I expected to have to explain at length. No need, as Rangers' plight had gone viral.

The London Olympics had just started but the barman had BBC Alba on! Suddenly, this Greek bar became Glebe Park, and a handful of Rangers fans watched what looked suspiciously like a football match. After four long months, The Journey was about to begin.

Maybe I was wrong to compare the day we went into admin to a family member being seriously ill, but that day in July was such a relief it was like seeing that family member leap out of their hospital bed and take the first few small steps to recovery. They might have been a shadow of their former selves, but that heart was still beating. Indeed, when Andy Little scored after four minutes it even seemed like watching great Rangers teams of the past, although the rest of that extra-time 'classic' was more a portent of what was to come on the park.

The ups and downs would be best illustrated by beating SPL leaders Motherwell in the League Cup as a third division team, and losing to Alloa in the Ramsdens Cup after being 2-0 up with 20 minutes to go.

The Journey took a little longer than expected, but we visited grounds we would never otherwise have experienced and hopefully as supporters we will have learned never to take our club, our stadium and our players for granted.

I have now seen Rangers play all 42 clubs in the SPFL (except Ross County, yet to visit Ibrox for a competitive match), and indeed win every single senior trophy and league division in Scotland.

Hopefully we will win the big three again soon, to shut the mouths of our enemies.

Yet for me that match against Brechin City will always be special, even if I was 5,000 miles away that day, because it was such a relief to finally be able to watch the Rangers again!

Ian Meechan, China

The only Rangers story I can tell you is how difficult it is getting to see a Gers game in north-east China. Thank goodness for kickass and some wee Scottish bloke who used to post *Sportscene* up on the web. I had to wait a week for the game as there was only one feed. Our internet is pants, 50 kb, and it took two days to upload!

The team had actually played the next game before I could watch the first one, so I switched off my Sky Sports, Rangers and BBC notifications so that I wouldn't find out the score, but it was all worth it.

I can't wait for the new season and it looks as though Celtic might think it'll be easy.

Mon the Gers and good luck with the book.

Ammy Singh, Australia

Having moved to Australia in January 2012, I had my return trip planned around the Rangers. Upon arriving back at Glasgow Airport on 2 January, I was met at the airport by a fellow Bear whom I had never met before. He not only bundled me and my baggage into his car, and drove us straight out to Dumbarton, but also gave me his highly sought after ticket to the game. It was a great day and a great win!

As was the Cowdenbeath match the following week, but the highlight was to be on the 16th when, as a Christmas present, I flew my lifelong friend up from Wales to attend our first Rangers match together. We both left the West Coast towns of Irvine and Troon in the late 80s and never did manage a game at Ibrox, until 16 January 2016 – that game against Livingston.

Thanks to the eagle eye and steady lens of Willie Vass, we have a lasting memory of our bucket list match!

Jim Bertram

In October 2012, I went on a trip to India with Punjabi Wolves to help build houses with the money we had raised during a rickshaw ride to Buckingham Palace for the Queen's Jubilee.

Myself and Stoke City fan, Gordon Walker, then came up with the idea of cycling from Stoke to Ibrox, a distance of 300 miles, in three days to raise money for both clubs' charity foundations.

We arrived at Ibrox on the last game of the season in April 2013 and received a standing ovation from a capacity crowd. It was amazing, and as a lifelong fan there was no better experience than cycling around Ibrox with fans cheering you.

It was breathtaking.

We continued this for three years and earlier this year we cycled from Inverness to Ibrox for the last game against Alloa, and what a way to finish after four years of doing this.

It has been such a journey, and we have had amazing support.

First team players and legends have supported our charity efforts.

Over 100 people have cycled in our challenges.

Two people have done the lot, Tony Proudman and James Bertram.

We have had over 500 people involved in fundraising efforts.

Over £70,000, including gift aid, has been raised for Rangers Charity Foundation and Stoke City Community Trust.

Rangers Charity Foundation has received £39,500.

Organising these events has taken a great deal of personal time, and for that I would like to thank my partner Jo Aston for her amazing support. We have made so many new friends and played a small part in helping change people's lives for the better.

Fraser Weir shows off his ticket collection – one from every away game!

The Results Archive

Season 2012/13

Scottish Third Division

11.08.12	Peterhead 2 Rangers 2	4,485
18.08.12	Rangers 5 East Stirling 1	49,118
26.08.12	Berwick Rangers 2 Rangers 2	4,140
02.09.12	Rangers 5 Elgin City 1	46,015
15.09.12	Annan Athletic 0 Rangers 0	2,517
23.09.12	Rangers 4 Montrose 1	45,081
06.10.12	Stirling Albion 1 Rangers 0	3,751
20.10.12	Rangers 2 Queen's Park 0	49,463
28.10.12	Clyde 0 Rangers 2	7,500
10.11.12	Rangers 2 Peterhead 0	48,407
17.11.12	East Stirling 2 Rangers 6	2,834
08.12.12	Rangers 2 Stirling Albion 0	49,913
15.12.12	Montrose 2 Rangers 4	4,205
18.12.12	Rangers 3 Annan Athletic 0	42,135
22.12.12	Elgin City 2 Rangers 6	3,448
26.12.12	Rangers 3 Clyde 0	47,463
29.12.12	Queen's Park 0 Rangers 1	30,117
02.01.13	Annan Athletic 1 Rangers 3	2,441
05.01.13	Rangers 1 Elgin City 1	46,406
12.01.13	Rangers 4 Berwick Rangers 2	44,976
20.01.13	Peterhead 0 Rangers 1	4,855
26.01.13	Rangers 1 Montrose 1	46,273

09.02.13	Rangers 4 Queen's Park 0	46,104
16.02.13	Clyde 1 Rangers 4	7,600
23.02.13	Berwick Rangers 1 Rangers 3	4,476
26.02.13	Stirling Albion 1 Rangers 1	3,707
02.03.13	Rangers 3 East Stirling 1	44,534
09.03.13	Rangers 1 Annan Athletic 2	34,441
16.03.13	Elgin City 0 Rangers 1	3,663
23.03.13	Rangers 0 Stirling Albion 0	44,608
30.03.13	Montrose 0 Rangers 0	4,686
07.04.13	Queen's Park 1 Rangers 4	11,492
13.04.13	Rangers 2 Clyde 0	44,453
20.04.13	Rangers 1 Peterhead 2	43,961
27.04.13	East Stirling 2 Rangers 4	2,885
04.05.13	Rangers 1 Berwick Rangers 0	50,048

Scottish League Cup

07.08.12 R1	Rangers 4 East Fife 0	38,160
30.08.12 R2	Rangers 3 Falkirk 0	26,450
26.09.12 R3	Rangers 2 Motherwell 0	29,413
31.10.12 QF	Rangers 0 Inverness Caley Th 3	28,033

Ramsdens Cup

29.07.12 R1	Brechin City 1 Rangers 2	4,123
21.08.12 R2	Falkirk 0 Rangers 1	6,747
18.09.12 QF	Rangers 2 Queen of the South 2 (QoS win pens)	23,932

Scottish Cup

29.09.12 R2	Forres Mechanics 0 Rangers 1	2,750

03.11.12 R3	Rangers 7 Alloa Athletic 0	25,478
02.12.12 R4	Rangers 3 Elgin City 0	23,195
02.02.13 R5	Dundee United 3 Rangers 0	9,564

Top Scorers:

26	Lee McCulloch
25	Andy Little
15	David Templeton
12	Dean Shiels
5	Robbie Crawford
4	Barrie McKay
4	Lee Wallace
3	Fraser Aird
3	Kevin Kyle
3	Lewis Macleod
3	Kal Naismith
2	Ian Black
2	Kyle Hutton
2	Fran Sandaza

Season 2013/14

Scottish League One

10.08.13	Rangers 4 Brechin City 1	44,380
17.08.13	Stranraer 0 Rangers 3	3,473
23.08.13	Airdrie 0 Rangers 6	9,044
31.08.13	Rangers 5 East Fife 0	42,870
14.09.13	Rangers 5 Arbroath 1	43,562
22.09.13	Forfar Athletic 0 Rangers 1	3,776
28.09.13	Rangers 8 Stenhousemuir 0	43,877
06.10.13	Ayr United 0 Rangers 2	8,968
19.10.13	Brechin City 3 Rangers 4	3,237
26.10.13	East Fife 0 Rangers 4	4,700

06.11.13	Rangers 3 Dunfermline Ath 1	43,082
09.11.13	Rangers 2 Airdrie 0	43,158
25.11.13	Arbroath 0 Rangers 3	3,912
03.12.13	Rangers 6 Forfar Athletic 1	38,745
07.12.13	Rangers 3 Ayr United 0	45,227
26.12.13	Rangers 1 Stranraer 1	45,462
30.12.13	Dunfermline Ath 0 Rangers 4	10,089
02.01.14	Airdrie 0 Rangers 1	6,552
05.01.14	Stenhousemuir 0 Rangers 2	2,546
11.01.14	Rangers 2 East Fife 0	42,182
20.01.14	Forfar Athletic 0 Rangers 2	3,067
25.01.14	Rangers 3 Arbroath 2	41,207
01.02.14	Rangers 2 Brechin City 1	40,577
15.02.14	Ayr United 0 Rangers 2	8,449
22.02.14	Rangers 3 Stenhousemuir 3	41,794
25.02.14	Stranraer 0 Rangers 2	3,024
01.03.14	East Fife 0 Rangers 1	4,020
12.03.14	Rangers 3 Airdrie 0	41,343
15.03.14	Rangers 2 Dunfermline Ath 0	44,110
23.03.14	Brechin City 1 Rangers 2	3,070
29.03.14	Arbroath 1 Rangers 2	3,400
15.04.14	Rangers 3 Forfar Athletic 0	39,704
19.04.14	Stenhousemuir 0 Rangers 4	2,767
22.04.14	Rangers 2 Ayr United 1	40,651
26.04.14	Rangers 3 Stranraer 0	46,093
03.05.14	Dunfermline Ath 1 Rangers 1	7,605

Ramsdens Cup

27.07.13 R1	Albion Rovers 0 Rangers 4	5,345
27.08.13 R2	Rangers 2 Berwick Rangers 0	16,097
17.09.13 QF	Queen of the South 0 Rangers 3	6,155
29.10.13 SF	Stenhousemuir 0 Rangers 1	2,338
06.04.14 F	Rangers 0 Raith Rovers 1 (AET) (at Easter Road)	19,983

Scottish League Cup

03.08.13 R1   Forfar Ath 2 Rangers 1 (AET)   4,079

Scottish Cup

01.11.13 R3	Rangers 3 Airdrie 0	22,533
30.11.13 R4	Falkirk 0 Rangers 2	6,228
07.02.14 R5	Rangers 4 Dunfermline Ath 0	19,396
09.03.14 QF	Rangers 1 Albion Rovers 1	23,976
18.03.14 QFR	Albion Rovers 0 Rangers 2	5,354
12.04.14 SF	Dundee United 3 Rangers 1	41,059

Top Scorers:

25	Jon Daly
18	Lee McCulloch
12	Bilel Mohsni
12	Nicky Law
11	Dean Shiels
9	Nicky Clark
7	Fraser Aird
7	David Templeton
6	Andy Little
5	Lewis Macleod
3	Ian Black
3	Steven Smith
3	Lee Wallace
2	Robbie Crawford

Season 2014/15

Scottish Championship

10.08.14	Rangers 1 Hearts 2	43,683
15.08.14	Falkirk 0 Rangers 2	6,927
23.08.14	Rangers 4 Dumbarton 1	31,175
30.08.14	Rangers 4 Queen of the South 2	31,815

12.09.14	Raith Rovers 0 Rangers 4	6,250
20.09.14	Alloa Athletic 1 Rangers 1	2,793
29.09.14	Rangers 1 Hibs 3	31,169
04.10.14	Livingston 0 Rangers 1	5,924
18.10.14	Rangers 6 Raith Rovers 1	33,956
25.10.14	Dumbarton 0 Rangers 3	1,850
04.11.14	Cowdenbeath 0 Rangers 3	3,919
08.11.14	Rangers 4 Falkirk 0	33,359
15.11.14	Rangers 1 Alloa Athletic 1	29,548
22.11.14	Hearts 2 Rangers 0	17,004
06.12.14	Rangers 1 Cowdenbeath 0	28,137
12.12.14	Queen of the South 2 Rangers 0	6,185
20.12.14	Rangers 2 Livingston 0	28,053
27.12.14	Hibs 4 Rangers 0	15,216
03.01.15	Rangers 3 Dumbarton 1	30,031
10.01.15	Alloa Athletic 0 Rangers 1	3,012
13.02.15	Rangers 0 Hibs 2	29,769
20.02.15	Raith Rovers 1 Rangers 2	4,604
27.02.15	Falkirk 1 Rangers 1	7,492
07.03.15	Cowdenbeath 0 Rangers 0	3,244
10.03.15	Rangers 1 Queen of the South 1	35,018
14.03.15	Rangers 1 Livingston 1	35,066
17.03.15	Rangers 2 Alloa Athletic 2	28,902
22.03.15	Hibs 0 Rangers 2	14,075
28.03.15	Rangers 4 Cowdenbeath 1	32,682
05.04.15	Rangers 2 Hearts 1	40,521
09.04.15	Queen of the South 3 Rangers 0	35,018
12.04.15	Rangers 4 Raith Rovers 0	31,427
15.04.15	Livingston 1 Rangers 1	4,345
18.04.15	Dumbarton 1 Rangers 3	1,766
25.04.15	Rangers 2 Falkirk 2	35,566
02.05.15	Hearts 2 Rangers 2	16,874

Premiership Play-Offs

09.05.15	QF	Queen of the South 1 Rangers 2	5,224
17.05.15	QF	Rangers 1 Queen of the South 1	48,035
20.05.15	SF	Rangers 2 Hibs 0	41,236
23.05.15	SF	Hibs 1 Rangers 0	14,742
28.05.15	F	Rangers 1 Motherwell 3	49,200
31.05.15	F	Motherwell 3 Rangers 0	9,220

Challenge Cup

05.08.14	R1	Rangers 2 Hibs 1 (AET)	18,138
18.08.14	R2	Rangers 8 Clyde 1	11,190
21.10.14	QF	East Fife 0 Rangers 2	1,827
03.12.14	SF	Alloa Athletic 3 Rangers 2	2,443

Scottish League Cup

26.08.14	R1	Queen's Park 1 Rangers 2	3,674
16.09.14	R2	Rangers 1 Inverness Caley Th 0	15,208
23.09.14	R3	Falkirk 1 Rangers 3	5,259
28.10.14	QF	Rangers 1 St Johnstone 0	13,023
01.02.15	SF	Celtic 2 Rangers 0	50,925

Scottish Cup

01.11.14	R3	Dumbarton 0 Rangers 1	1,878
30.11.14	R4	Rangers 3 Kilmarnock 0	14,412
08.02.15	R5	Rangers 1 Raith Rovers 2	11,422

Top Scorers:

13	Nicky Law
10	Kris Boyd
9	Nicky Clark
9	Kenny Miller
9	Haris Vuckic
8	Lewis Macleod
6	Lee McCulloch
5	Darren McGregor
5	Dean Shiels
4	Jon Daly
4	Lee Wallace
3	Ian Black
3	David Templeton
2	Fraser Aird
2	Ryan Hardie
2	Marius Zaliukas

Season 2015/16

Scottish Championship

07.08.15	Rangers 3 St Mirren 1	49,216
16.08.15	Alloa Athletic 1 Rangers 5	3,047
23.08.15	Rangers 1 Hibs 0	49,220
30.08.15	Queen of the South 1 Rangers 5	5,858
05.09.15	Rangers 5 Raith Rovers 0	44,050
12.09.15	Rangers 3 Livingston 0	44,832
19.09.15	Dumbarton 1 Rangers 2	1,978
27.09.15	Morton 0 Rangers 4	7,392
03.10.15	Rangers 3 Falkirk 1	45,135
17.10.15	Rangers 2 Queen of the South 1	44,133
25.10.15	St Mirren 0 Rangers 1	5,477
01.11.15	Hibs 2 Rangers 1	14,412
07.11.15	Rangers 4 Alloa Athletic 0	43,242
21.11.15	Livingston 1 Rangers 1	6,505
01.12.15	Rangers 4 Dumbarton 0	37,182
12.12.15	Rangers 2 Morton 2	41,816
19.12.15	Falkirk 2 Rangers 1	7,488
28.12.15	Rangers 4 Hibs 2	49,995
02.01.16	Dumbarton 0 Rangers 6	1,894
16.01.16	Rangers 4 Livingston 1	42,906
25.01.16	Morton 0 Rangers 2	5,778
30.01.16	Rangers 1 Falkirk 0	46,980

02.02.16	Raith Rovers 0 Rangers 1	5,493	
13.02.16	Alloa Athletic 1 Rangers 1	3,100	
21.02.16	Queen of the South 0 Rangers 1	5,449	
27.02.16	Rangers 1 St Mirren 0	46,366	
01.03.16	Rangers 2 Raith Rovers 0	40,662	
11.03.16	Rangers 3 Morton 1	45,072	
18.03.16	Falkirk 3 Rangers 2	7,804	
26.03.16	Rangers 4 Queen of the South 3	46,117	
02.04.16	Raith Rovers 3 Rangers 3	6,943	
05.04.16	Rangers 1 Dumbarton 0	48,568	
20.04.16	Hibs 3 Rangers 2	12,231	
23.04.16	Rangers 1 Alloa Athletic 1	50,349	
26.04.16	Livingston 1 Rangers 0	5,021	
01.05.16	St Mirren 2 Rangers 2	5,933	

Petrofac Training Cup

25.07.15 R1	Hibs 2 Rangers 6	11,225	
19.08.15 R2	Ayr United 0 Rangers 2	7,468	
20.10.15 QF	Rangers 1 Livingston 0	17,836	
28.11.15 SF	Rangers 4 St Mirren 0	22,369	
10.04.16 F	Rangers 4 Peterhead 0	48,133	

Scottish League Cup

02.08.15 R1	Rangers 3 Peterhead 0	25,608	
26.08.15 R2	Airdrie 0 Rangers 5	7,006	
22.09.15 R3	Rangers 1 St Johnstone 3	27,094	

Scottish Cup

10.01.16 R4	Rangers 5 Cowdenbeath 1	20,915	
06.02.16 R5	Rangers 0 Kilmarnock 0	33,581	
16.02.16 R5R	Kilmarnock 1 Rangers 2	13,179	
05.03.16 QF	Rangers 4 Dundee 0	30,944	
17.04.16 SF	Rangers 2 Celtic 2 (AET) (Rangers 5-4 pens)	50,069	
21.05.16 F	Rangers 2 Hibs 3 (AET)	50,701	

Top Scorers:

28	Martyn Waghorn
20	Kenny Miller
15	James Tavernier
12	Jason Holt
9	Andy Halliday
9	Barrie McKay
9	Lee Wallace
6	Nicky Clark
5	Harry Forrester
3	Michael O'Halloran
3	Dean Shiels